HOPE

for a

BROKEN HEART

Powerful Stories of Healing
After the Death of a Child

LINDA D. STIRLING

Hope for a Broken Heart
Powerful Stories of Healing After the Death of a Child

Linda D. Stirling

© 2014 by Linda D. Stirling
ISBN 978-1497464094

Printed in the United States of America

Scripture taken from the Holy Bible, New International Translation, NIV, copyright © 1973, 1978, 1984, 2010 by Biblica, Inc., and from the New King James Version, copyright © 1979, 1980, 1982 by Thomas Nelson, Inc. Used by permission. All rights reserved worldwide.

Book Cover and Project Manager: Marcia Ramsland www.organizingpro.com
Editor: Mike Yorkey www.mikeyorkey.com
Cover and Interior Design: Eva Hill www.urickdesign.com

To access more information for mothers who would like support following the death of a child, please visit www.umbrellaministriesSD.com.

For bulk purchases of *Hope for a Broken Heart,* please contact Linda D. Stirling at www.hopeforabrokenheart.com

FOREWORD

By Ken and Marjorie Blanchard

Heartbreak can happen in an instant. An accident, a suicide, or a phone call that a loved one has passed away sweeps life off its foundation and hurdles us into despair. The heartache of tending to a family member dying from a prolonged disease can crush our spirit and cause profound sadness and depression. Our home burned to the ground with all of our life's possessions. We, too, mourned a loss of history and beauty that had surrounded our family for decades. Life's tragedies come in many forms, but the death of a child is an experience beyond human understanding. The natural order of our expectations is turned upside down. How can anyone ever cope with such a loss?

Linda Stirling has been our friend and advisor, as well as a board member of the Lead Like Jesus ministry, for almost twenty years. It was during a filmed interview with Linda for a series on talking and walking your faith in business that we first heard about her son Jeff's death and its impact on this then-single mother's life. Linda is passionate about coming alongside others whose lives have been crushed by loss, knowing that her life experience can help lead them out of the valley of the shadow of death toward a new life. This is the mission of her book, Hope for a Broken Heart.

Linda and the mothers whose stories she has written about know firsthand the struggle to survive after the death of a child. Their stories tell of pain and questioning through life's worst experience. In Linda's relating of each unique circumstance and the journey of each mother from devastation to newfound life, the pathway out of darkness is revealed. Choosing to make the life of their child meaningful after death brought God's hope and comfort to these mothers. They came to realize the futility of self-help and the peace that comes from God-help.

Each of these twelve stories clearly demonstrates how our incredible God visibly reaches into life's most devastating circumstances with His healing touch. Wow! Through tears to triumphs, this book delivers on its promise of hope. It will help you deal with any major pain you are experiencing presently and prepare you to handle any significant setback you might have to contend with in the future. When our home was destroyed by fire, we immediately turned to God. We knew we could not lean on our own understanding and He carried us through.

Thanks, Linda, for reminding us that we have a Shepherd who knows and cares about the details of our lives. In the toughest of circumstances, we can recognize that there is hope beyond ourselves. The stories in Hope for a Broken Heart lead us to that Hope that brings joy back into our lives and a purpose for our future.

Ken Blanchard
Coauthor, *The One Minute Manager* and *Lead Like Jesus*
Cofounder, The Ken Blanchard Companies

Marjorie Blanchard
Coauthor, *Leading at a Higher Level* and *Working Well*
Cofounder, The Ken Blanchard Companies

TABLE OF CONTENTS

Section Three: Turning Loss into Legacy

WORD FROM THE AUTHOR

*"I am a little pencil in the hand of a writing God
who is sending a love letter to the world."*

—Mother Teresa

It's no small miracle that this book is in your hands today. Having experienced the death of my oldest son, Jeff, at age nineteen, I know the fog that enshrouds the mind when grieving such a devastating loss. The ability to carry on a conversation, absorb well-intentioned comments of friends and family, or focus on the future became mighty chores. There were times when getting off the couch signaled a major achievement. I felt incapable of accomplishing anything. And yet, after a time, I was inspired to write a book of hope which has somehow found its way into your life.

Gathered here are stories from mothers who found the strength and courage to rise up from the depths of despair to discover purpose in their lives following the deaths of their children. The continuum of healing is unique to their circumstance, time being irrelevant on the pathway out of debilitating despair. For those of us who've lost a loved one, this is a lifetime journey.

Woven through each page of these heart-wrenching losses, you will find threads of hope for you, whether you are a mother, father, friend, or family member. Hope grows more apparent with each nuance of their unique stories, relating their path from the deepest anguish to an inspiration to live life anew.

We know, dear reader, our lives will never be the same. Strength develops slowly. It will enter your mind, heart, and body as you hear from mothers who want to share hope and a future beyond your loved one's death.

Healing is not the same as forgetting. Each mother included here was eager to tell the story of her child's life and yes, their death. Like my Jeff, these were vibrant young lives whose smiles and quirks, devilishness and promise live on in our memories, in our tributes, and in our own life's purpose. As each mother grasped the source of comfort and was able to turn her head toward the future, healing took on a purpose.

Read with an eye for how God intervenes through coincidences, unique circumstances, visions, dreams, and internally discernible voices—situations that could only be explained as God working in disguise. In each chapter, mark in the margin with an asterisk or a cross these God moments, orchestrated by Him to reassure you that He is beside you, behind you, and going in front of you to bring you peace and comfort. When doubt arises, return to your notations and find confirmation that GOD IS WITH YOU in your loss.

You have been prayed for since the day this book was conceived. In addition to reading *Hope for a Broken Heart,* I urge you to read Scripture. Stand on the promises of God's faithfulness in times of sorrow. Grasp your Creator's thoughts toward you, and know His comforting heart.

The following chapters will show you how grief transitions us from a lifeless existence toward life-sustaining hope that otherwise would have been elusive. These honest and real stories will help carry you through life's most devastating loss.

Let me say a prayer for you before you begin reading. Pray

with me now for your aching heart to be open to the healing that's possible after life's most crushing losses.

Dear God,

Bless these grieving souls as they seek inspiration for their lives. Let the words written here glorify You and demonstrate Your desire for them to know Your love and purpose for their lives. Bring to each reader calm, quiet, and peaceful periods in your presence as you faithfully did for each mother in these hope-filled stories. Heal these broken hearts wherever they are on their journey from being lost to living joyfully. Amen.

Caring for you,
Linda D. Stirling

THE JOURNEY

1

Walking Out of the Valley

A Psalm of Healing for Grieving Parents: The Author's Personal Story

Here we go again, I sighed sadly, thinking of what lay ahead for another grieving family.

The chaplain from the San Diego Fire and Rescue Department was on the phone, asking if I might accompany him when he returned a pair of shoes requested by a mother whose eleven-year-old boy had died the night before in a boating accident.

I knew why the chaplain had called me. We were acquainted with each other because he knew I had lost my nineteen-year-old son following the crash of a small single-engine plane. Having been a resource to hurting parents periodically over the years, this was another one of those heart-breaking occasions that is every parent's worst fear: the death of a child.

The story of the San Diego Bay Parade of Lights incident was in the morning newspaper. News stories about tragic losses always catch my eye when sipping my first cup of coffee before leaving for work.

In this calamitous accident, a U.S. Coast Guard boat, rushing to assist a grounded sailboat that radioed for help, had collided with a private yacht with two families onboard who were watching the festive parade of lighted boats. When the thirty-three-foot Coast Guard cutter racing at nearly 50 miles per hour slammed into the anchored, twenty-four-foot yacht, the boy was killed instantly while ten others suffered injuries. Knowing that I too had lost my son suddenly, the chaplain thought I might offer comfort to this heartbroken mother by bringing her son's shoes to her door. The shoes had been on the boat deck during the collision and tumbled into the water.

What could it be about these shoes? I wondered. I thought back to how the sorting of my son's clothing was not a task assigned to me following his death. My son Jeff was plagued with stinky feet, and if I had folded the clothes left on the floor of his messy bedroom, the distinctive smell of my son's shoes might have brought Jeff closer to me in that incredible void of his absence. Would I have kept his shoes?

I desperately wanted to hug this grieving mother, to look her in the eyes and say I understood her pain and was there for her, but she requested that her son's shoes be left on the front porch step. Inside one shoe, I asked the chaplain to tuck a poem I had written, inspired by this mother's desire to have her son's special shoes.

This particular poem had crept into my heart when I thoughtfully considered how I might bring comfort to this devastated family. My words poured out onto the paper, flowing from my experienced heart, remembering how a life can vanish in an unexpected instant.

HIS SHOES

When first I saw his little feet
An infant so divine,
I marveled at this precious gift,
This darling boy of mine.

They grew so fast those little feet,
They soon found strength to stand.
Before too long with confidence sure
Into the world he ran.

Through puddles slick and mud so thick
How boys do love such muck.
A child's play each and every day,
'Til he finally found the puck.

Walking shoes to racing skates,
Hockey was his calling.
Those growing feet had their wings
Their goal was that of scoring.

How big those feet may have grown,
It's not for us to know.
Now his field is dusted with gold
And a different wind does blow.

Swept away, that life so prime,
We hardly believe it's true.
All the promise, times to come
Seem lost, what can we do?

The painful time of letting go
Does not mean giving away.
Forever he's a treasured son
As that he will always stay.

In photos, friends, stories, thoughts,
With us will always be,
That little boy's gleeful smile,
Forever, our Anthony.

The Holy Spirit, comforter
Brings healing power to us,
The void that those little feet have left
Can be filled as we learn to trust.

God's heartfelt Love is with you now
His right hand holds yours fast
He knows your loss, He gave *His* son,
If only we can grasp—

His purpose true, for life eternal,
A heaven not on earth.
His feet have walked the path we tread,
Death leads us to rebirth.

Writing the poem and stepping into this family's devastation took me to a dark place where I least liked to go—recalling my own son's death. The accidental death of a child is like a lightening bolt that pierces the heart and changes the landscape of your life forever.

When your firstborn child is swaddled and gently placed in your arms, not for a second do you ponder the limited number of years given to this precious life. When my oldest of two sons was born, I never imagined that I'd know Jeff for only nineteen years, even though in the first weeks of his infancy, Jeff was challenged with a malfunctioning pyloric valve that wouldn't allow food to pass from the stomach to the duodenum.

Doctors determined his deteriorating condition would require immediate surgery. Imagine trusting this little one to the hands of a surgeon, wondering if he would survive the procedure. Thankfully, all went well, and Jeff was good as new. With grateful anticipation, we eagerly moved forward, fully expecting a lifetime with Jeffrey. But God had different plans for Jeff—and for us.

Precocious from a Young Age

A towhead at birth, Jeff was full of exuberance from the day I brought him home from the hospital. Before his first birthday, Jeff surprised us and spoke in complete sentences. By the age of two, his incredible little voice would blast out "God Bless America" and "You're a Grand Old Flag," and he could also recite an impassioned Lord's Prayer from beginning to end. At five years of age, Jeff made a big decision. After church one Sunday morning, he came running out of his Sunday school class, proclaiming he had Jesus in his heart.

I bent down and looked into his beaming eyes. "Really? How do you know?" I asked.

"There was this puppet, and he said Jesus wants to come into our lives, and all we have to do is ask Him into our heart," he replied. "So I invited Him in, Mom, and He's living right here forever!"

With a huge grin, Jeff pressed both his little hands over his heart, and I can still picture the scene today. I have rewound the memory of that morning many times over the years, each time with the hope and the promise of Jeff's eternity and God's hand on his young life that day.

Jeff's best year in school was kindergarten. He excelled in recess and other sports activities, but focus strained his bright mind. He struggled with dyslexia, not commonly diagnosed in his early years. When all is not right with the brain's ability to read and retain, one's school experience can be like drowning in a pool with everyone watching you struggle. Bright, athletic, handsome, and funny, but lacking the emotional balance that comes from feeling capable, Jeff grappled with self-control and relationships at school and in the neighborhood.

Emerging Passion

Capturing the heart and passion of this challenged child was the experience of flying, which he was introduced to by my father, a licensed pilot, when Jeff was three years old. One time, we met his granddad at Palomar Airport in Carlsbad, where he and Jeff hopped into his private plane and flew "touch and goes," a practice that kept pilots current with their flying requirements.

Jeff's auntie, my sister Patti, was also a pilot, so between her and my father, Jeff had plenty of opportunities to be in the air throughout his childhood. It seemed for Jeff that Earth was a weighty place to be, while flying allowed him to soar above his troubles.

At fifteen, Jeff enrolled in flight school. At the time, we were living in Hailey, Idaho, a wooded community just outside the famous Sun Valley ski resort. The small regional airport was located at the end of a valley where the mountains fell away to a vast flat terrain, perfect for learning to fly.

After passing the exams—not an easy feat, due to his learning disabilities—he was ready to solo. Jeff was prepared. He wore his favorite red crew neck shirt, ready for the traditional "cutting of the cloth" when a successful solo was completed. My husband, Dick, and I watched from the ground, two proud parents believing this boy had found his calling. On that sunny afternoon in May, he passed all aspects of flight training with proverbial flying colors.

But all was not soaring in Jeff's life. Erratic behavior caused us to suspect drug use. One Saturday night when Jeff came home with glassy eyes and an uncertain gait, Dick and I informed him that we wanted him to take a drug test. At first, he rebelled, prompting us to inform him that we would not allow him in the cockpit again. Reluctantly, he took the drug test, but when he failed, Jeff's wings were clipped, which kept him from the very thing that made him feel capable.

Especially difficult for Jeff was accepting the fragmentation of his family that came when his father and I divorced. Jeff was eighteen. He and his younger brother Greg chose to move with me from Hailey, where we had resided for most of their lives, to San Diego. My ex-husband stayed behind in Idaho.

Step of Independence

After a tumultuous high school senior year in San Diego, Jeff was determined to try a term at an Oregon flight training school. I'll never forget when he packed up for the drive to Eugene, site of the ground school training.

At the time, I was new in my career as a financial advisor with Merrill Lynch, barely making ends meet with a meager

$300-a-month child support check and a low starting salary.
Hesitant to leave my job or my younger son, Greg, I determined
that this was his adventure and I would not be driving with him
to Eugene. He was angry at my decision as well as scared of this
enormous step of independence, however.

The Saturday morning Jeff was to leave was rainy and we all slept
in. He had spent the prior evening with his high school friends and
appeared red-eyed and tired at the kitchen table. I had prepared a
favorite breakfast for his departure, but his grumpy mood was not
elevated by the meal. He trudged back upstairs to retrieve his suitcase,
bumping the wall as he dragged his clothes down to the garage level.

"Careful," I commented in my usual instructive tone.

"Who cares? It's not our place," he said, referring to the fact it
was a rental unit.

"We still need to take care of this place," I continued, although I
realized the bumping of the walls reflected something more serious
than just thoughtlessness.

"Can I help?" I asked.

"Mom, what difference does it make? I'm out of here and out of
your way!" he yelled emotionally.

"Jeff, we're going to miss you so much, but I know you're going
to do well in the training program," I said, trying to bolster these
last moments between us. I could tell his fears were the same as
mine. We were separating, and it was scary. At that moment, I
knew my child wanted me to be with him during this transition,
but I wasn't going on the journey.

As he turned to drive away, I rushed over to hug him. But his
bitterness was apparent as he slammed the door. At that moment,

watching his white truck disappear around the corner, I knew I should have gone. I was in tears and miserable.

Jeff was not ready for the independence he had claimed. He wasn't in Eugene very long when he stopped attending classes at his flight school and fell into depression. His father and I made the difficult decision that Jeff needed to take a step back while he sorted through what he wanted to do with his life. Jeff's dad drove to Oregon, and together they caravanned back to Idaho, where Jeff lived with his father while he tried to figure out what to do next.

Before the divorce, Jeff had attended Wood River High School for a couple of years and his friendships in this rural area were quickly rekindled. Jeff applied for a job at the local airport that serviced the Sun Valley resort area and was hired at a private-plane facility, where he towed planes and prepped them for service, and, at times, fulfilled his love of flying.

Seeking to Impress His Date

Typical of a nineteen-year-old young man, Jeff enjoyed the company of attractive young women. In an attempt to impress one potential girlfriend, he invited her—on their first date—to take an afternoon flight into the majestic mountains surrounding the Wood River Valley. Jeff told the young woman, Joy, that he could rent a light airplane for the afternoon.

Excited to see the turning leaves and fall landscape from high above the Wood River Valley, Joy agreed to meet Jeff at Hailey's Friedman Memorial Airport that beautiful October afternoon. Jeff's father's Cessna 182 was undergoing maintenance repairs, so they took off in a Cherokee 180, a plane in which Jeff had only a few hours flying time and which lacked the equipment similar to his father's.

Jeff flew north out of Hailey into the Sawtooth Mountain Range. The aspen leaves had transformed themselves into bright yellow shimmering hands, waving with the wind that blew into the canyons. If Jeff and Joy looked close enough, they could see elk and deer scampering across meadows and throughout the rugged terrain.

Attempting a closer view of a remote draw of mountains, Jeff maneuvered the plane along the ridges that bordered Corral Creek. As he turned, he suddenly noticed a higher ridgeline of jagged-toothed mountains at the end of the valley. Recognizing immediately that he was boxed in, Jeff banked the plane sharply, pushing the throttle forward and lifting the plane as precipitously as he might without causing a stall.

The little Cherokee did not have the thrust of the more familiar Cessna. Seeing that he was suddenly in a tight spot, Jeff coaxed the Cherokee upward, hoping he had enough lift to carry the plane over the ridgeline. When seconds passed and it became apparent that he *wasn't* going to make it over the mountain, he banked again, attempting to circle out of the canyon. That's when his wing struck a large tree limb, and the plane wrapped around and crashed into the side of the mountain, landing on its side.

Wreckage was strewn everywhere. Miraculously, there was no fire. Joy was strapped in the passenger seat, which buckled forward with the momentum of the crash. Joy was knocked unconscious.

The story was different for my son. He was not wearing his safety harness, and when the plane struck the ground, he was thrown from the plane. Jeff died on impact.

A hiker in the vicinity saw the plane go down, crashing into the mountainside. Running at top speed, he reached the accident scene quickly. He determined that my son was dead, but Joy was still breathing. He released her from her seatbelt, but her legs were trapped under the weight of her seat. Slowly and carefully, he extricated her limbs and gently placed Joy on the ground, covering her with his jacket. Assessing her situation as critical, he decided the best way to save her life was to run for help. He retraced his path to a remote cabin at the base of the mountain, where he contacted the local Search and Rescue operation. A helicopter was dispatched in the fading sunlight, and rescuers airlifted the unconscious young woman to the medical facilities in Sun Valley.

Joy survived, thank God.

My son did not.

The Horrible News

Another twelve hours would pass before I heard the cataclysmic news.

I was at my San Diego home, fully dressed at 7 a.m. and getting ready to leave for the airport. I had a 9 o'clock flight to New York's JFK Airport, where I had a business meeting the following day.

The phone rang, which was unusual, given the early hour. My ex-husband was on the line.

"Linda, something happened."

"What?" My heart leaped into my throat. I knew it had to be something serious since Dick was calling so early.

"We lost Jeff last night in a plane crash. I didn't want to call you until authorities confirmed the situation." Then Dick could no longer speak. I was at a loss for words. As the news began to dawn on me, I screamed, "NO, NO, NO!" My screams of pain and shouting were so loud that a neighbor called the police, believing I was being harmed.

I started gasping for breaths of air as waves of shock came over me. My world spun, and I did my best to keep from collapsing to the ground. My son was dead! It couldn't be true!

After Dick's phone call, I groped to make sense of this tragic news and kept telling myself this couldn't be happening. Then I realized this was reality and the first thing I needed to do was wake Greg, then sixteen at the time, and share the crushing news that he had just lost his older brother, his best friend. This was an indelible moment.

The next week was a blur. Flying to Idaho with Greg, just putting one foot in front of the other was accomplished only with the help of friends and family. The protective fog of disbelief cushioned the bleakness of each waking moment. Sleep came only with help. Darkness wrapped everything in a gray blanket of despair. A pastor's prayer, friends' generous help, and strong, bear-like hugs from family helped us walk through that devastating week.

Seeing the body was not an option. We had Jeff cremated, and his ashes were flown over the river behind our Idaho house and deposited where he loved to fish and hunt. After a gut-wrenching service, Greg and I made our way back to San Diego in a self-preserving emotional fog. Friends encircled us with love, food, and fond memories. It was all so unreal.

I knew my life and the lives of those closest to me would be forever changed.

Getting Back to Life

Greg, a junior in high school, spent the first day with me at home. We walked and talked and cried and laughed. Greg told me stories about some of Jeff's crazy stunts that had escaped my disciplined eye.

But then came the next day. Nothing had changed. I awakened to the same reality of a broken heart. At breakfast, my sixteen-year-old son made an insightful statement: "Mom, we've got to get back to life. I need to go to school, and you need to go to work. We have to start living again."

Every day for several weeks, my routine was the same. I would cry myself to work in the morning, do my job, cry myself home in the evening, and then be strong for Greg. My younger son wanted life back to "normal," but I knew there was no more normal.

One memorable day when I was caught in five o'clock traffic, I pounded on the steering wheel of the car, tears flowing down my cheeks, and demanded aloud of the void around me: "How could you have done this, Jeff? You were such a good pilot!"

As though a voice were coming out of the car radio, the words came unmistakably to my mind: "Mom, don't be mad at me. I didn't mean to."

My heart melted. Have you heard your child ever say with sweet sincerity, "I didn't mean to, Mom. Don't be mad?"

The tight ball of anger trapped in my heart broke open, and I answered Jeff out loud. "Oh, I know you didn't mean to. I'm not mad at you. Really."

The destructive weight of poisonous anger was lifted from my heart. Had I heard his voice? No. But my heart needed to be freed from the crippling, life-crushing hold that anger had on my life.

As I continued to sit in the maze of traffic, I had this feeling that God wanted me to start listening to Him. I reached in the side pocket of my car door and pulled out the only available tape, which was entitled "A Shepherd's Walk" on Psalm 23 by Dr. Lloyd John Ogilvie from the First Presbyterian Church of Hollywood, California.

I had memorized the passage of Scripture, which speaks of "the valley of the shadow of death," as a young girl in Sunday school. In my personal valley that very day, Dr. Ogilvie's words put me on a path of healing that rescued me from despair, guided by a shepherd's staff and the Shepherd's incredible love for His flock.

As soon as I was home, I made a 3x5 card for each day of the week, each with a Psalm 23 verse and strengthening message provided to me that night in the car. When the fog of despair would again descend, as it did for months, I would repeat that portion of God's Word out loud for the day.

Repetition through the weeks was like a workout routine for my heart. It's said that time heals our wounds, but I didn't find that time was providing any relief from my brokenness and despair. But after meditating on God's words of tender mercy through Psalm 23, I truly became stronger and more resilient. These promises of the Helper became an elixir of joy that could only come from God.

Turning to God had not been my habit, but through my son's death, His path for my life became a ministry, accepting His plan to use every aspect of my life for another's good will. Power and joy came in the reading and I ventured into more of His healing scriptures. His strength and His vision equipped me to look upward and my life began to heal. Psalm 23 provided a daily adventure with God as my partner.

As I've shared my story over the years, God placed other grieving parents in my path. I sat with, listened to, cried with, and hugged these hurting mothers and fathers. Then I followed a calling to begin the San Diego chapter of Umbrella Ministries for mothers who had experienced the death of a child. If you are one of those mothers or fathers, or a close friend or family member, please know that I have written this book for you. In future chapters, you will read about how other parents dealt with the loss of a child and what they went through. Learn from them.

So as we begin, grab His hand and walk with Him. You'll find each day becomes a victory. But first, turn the page and take a seven-day walk with the Shepherd.

Thoughts to Ponder

- If you could change one situation you are remembering about your child, what would it be? Write a letter to your child as though that circumstance was changed.

- What healing instances have you experienced since the death of your child? Journal those experiences daily.

- Begin to read a modern version of the Bible, such as the New Living Translation or the New International Version. Underline verses that comfort your heart and lead you on a path of healing. Write them on a 3x5 card. Reread them often.

The Author's Story

In the year prior to Jeff's death, I divorced and moved from Sun Valley, Idaho, to San Diego with my two teenaged sons. That same year, my mother died of cancer—just three months prior to Jeff's accident. Anger and grief overwhelmed my life until I was confronted with the heart-changing experience of healing through Psalm 23.

Formerly a teacher at the elementary and junior high level, I journeyed through the devastation of my son's death and that traumatic year to launch a new career as a financial advisor. Four years after Jeff's death I married Larry Stirling, now retired from his position as a Superior Court Judge. Currently I continue to develop my practice as a wealth management advisor, recently forming a partnership with my son Greg at UBS Financial Services INC, with offices in San Diego and Sun Valley, Idaho. Greg's marriage provided us with one of the joys of our lives, granddaughter Madelyn.

My life continues to be blessed by the brave women who come together at the Umbrella Ministries' monthly meetings in my home. Their stories of loss and healing touch my heart. Through the sharing of personal triumphs, others in the group find a helping hand guiding them forward along their path of out of despair.

Joy, who survived multiple surgeries following the Jeff's plane crash, now uses her experience as she works with other survivors of traumatic experience.

To access information for mothers who would like support or to contact me, please go to www.hopeforabrokenheart.com

The Seven-Day Walk with the Shepherd
Psalm 23 for the Grieving Parent

For me, connecting with God through the daily habit of reading His wise counsel developed within me the seeds of hope, the buds of courage, and a light that allowed joy to once again enter my life. The Bible stories of the Old Testament and the life of Jesus in the New Testament encouraged me to become a new person, not by my own resolve, but through the strength that comes in the promises He has penned for us to stand upon.

PSALM 23

The LORD is my shepherd, I shall not want.
He makes me lie down in green pastures;
He leads me beside quiet waters.
He restores my soul;
He guides me in the paths of righteousness for His name's sake.
Even though I walk through the valley of the shadow of death,
I fear no evil, for You are with me;
Your rod and Your staff, they comfort me.
You prepare a table before me in the presence of my enemies;
You have anointed my head with oil; My cup overflows.
Surely goodness and mercy will follow me all the days of my life,
And I will dwell in the house of the LORD forever.

—Psalm 23 (NKJV)

Monday: "The Lord is my Shepherd" (Psalm 23:1)

To me, that meant the Lord was at work for me. He knows me like no other and therefore knows exactly what I need for my child's welfare, my job, and my personal health. Every Monday in my planner, I would write: *The Lord is my Shepherd*. He's out there bringing in just the right client and the right relationships. God has been so good as to usher wonderful people to my door in my personal as well as professional life. What a Partner I have—and so do you.

Tuesday: "I shall not want" (Psalm 23:1-2)

The Lord will provide for me. He feeds me and quiets my anxiety. He looks ahead and prepares the way. I have seen God's supply coming to me daily. Always in the nick of time, when credit can only be given to God, my human need is met. What a perfect God, with His perfect timing and the perfect solution. I shall not want. Believe it—He has promised it.

Wednesday: "The Lord will keep me going; He restores my soul" (Psalm 23:3)

Oh, did I need that promise that miserable day on Interstate 5, as well as today. The example that created the clearest picture for me is that of the tending shepherd. When the sheep would lie down in the damp grass, their thick wool would be so wet and heavy they would be unable to stand up again on their own. The shepherd would literally grab hold of the wool on their back and gently lift them onto their feet. Can you relate as I did? The Shepherd repeatedly lifted my heart out of the darkness and showed me new opportunities and new beginnings. He restored my soul.

Thursday: "The Lord will guide me" (Psalm 23:3)

The paths of righteousness were not necessarily my walkway at that time. We often look for love in all the wrong places, yet every Thursday when I reread this verse, I was reminded that I had a leader who wanted to set me on the path of righteousness for His name's sake.

Friday: "The Lord will protect me" (Psalm 23:4)

The imagery of the staff of the shepherd demonstrates how God is truly there each and every day to protect me from the predators of lust, greed, fear, and vanity. Yet the staff is also used to prod, to keep me going and moving on with life. At first, depression and introspection were immobilizing. But then I was prodded to call a friend, read the Bible, volunteer at church, or play tennis with my son Greg. Such shepherding lifted my fear of failure, bankruptcy, and life without a soul mate. The Lord protected me. God's protective rod and staff got me off my duff and moving in the right direction.

Saturday: "The Lord will heal me" (Psalm 23:5)

Physically, mentally and emotionally, God wants us to surrender our wounds and emotional sores. When the healing involves God, the results include miracles. The dark valley of depression is the enemy of our soul. Each day I would visualize Him anointing me with the most precious oils of His love, holding my right hand and drawing me out of the shadows of anger and fear to the comforting still waters and beautiful green pastures. He will mend my broken heart.

Sunday: "The Lord will pursue me" (Psalm 23:6)

Surely goodness and mercy shall follow me all the days of my life. God is relentless. My life is full of miracles, little ones and big ones, because He never gave up on me. When problems present themselves, as they continue to do, I am moved to start looking for the Shepherd's way.

I do not believe God allowed my son to die so that I would learn these lessons. Jeff is in heaven, possibly the angels' flight control officer, as I like to think. His struggles are over; he's on the other side.

Here on earth, I know that God wants goodness and mercy in my life. In spite of my tendency to mess it up on my own, God will pursue, prod, heal, protect, guide, provide, and lift me up when I get down.

* * *

Isn't it amazing that thousands of years ago David was inspired by God to write this Psalm just for me—and for you—to show us the way to triumph over tragedy and to walk the adventurous life with Him? The habit of reading the scriptures and walking with the Shepherd takes just one day at a time, so go on a stroll with the Shepherd.

I invite you to take that first step of healing today.

2

Passing It On

A Child's Heart Failure Inspires a Personal Outreach

When Kent Wright proposed to his girlfriend, Jesse Saar, he joked that she should think twice about her acceptance.

Why? Because for the last fifty years, no female children had been born into his family. If Jesse's hope was to raise a little girl in pink, she might be sorely disappointed, Kent told her.

Despite the daunting odds of ever having a girl, Jesse laughed and eagerly accepted Kent's marriage proposal. A year after their wedding, their first baby boy, Jarrett, was born. Several years later, Jesse became pregnant again and prepared herself to deliver their second son. (The couple had asked not to be told the baby's sex during ultrasound recordings.) Toxemia in the late stages of her pregnancy, however, required a Caesarian section to be scheduled for the baby's birth.

Both sides of the family were on hand for the delivery, ready to celebrate another grandchild. When baby Kylie Nicole was presented, Kent pumped his fists and the nurses cheered when a girl had been born. Jesse, in disbelief, insisted her husband check their baby again.

"You sure it's a girl?" she questioned. Her mind was filled with names for boys, and there certainly were no frilly pink outfits awaiting this baby's arrival at their home.

Within a few minutes of Kylie's birth, however, Kent and Jesse's collective joy turned to fear. Baby Kylie was struggling for breath.

Doctors quickly determined that her aorta and pulmonary arteries were reversed, and a tiny hole was discovered in her heart. Because Kylie's arteries were transposed, the blood flow to the heart was interrupted. Any blood coming back from the body was low on oxygen.

The decision was made to operate on the infant girl. The following morning, surgeons inserted a balloon catheter to open a hole between the upper chambers of Kylie's heart, which would allow blood to flow back and forth, temporarily ensuring her survival.

A Record of Events

Kylie rallied and gained strength. A month after her birth, she was scheduled for open heart surgery to further reverse the arteries and close the holes. Her mother kept a diary of her experiences over the course of the next month of Kylie's hospitalization.

Monday, February 17: Kent and I checked Kylie in today. They had to do all sorts of tests to make sure Kylie was ready for surgery. Everything went well and all systems are good to go for tomorrow.

Tuesday, February 18: I remember when I had to hand over my beautiful baby girl to the nurse, who wheeled her to the operating room. I thought it was the hardest thing I would ever have to do in my life. I realized it could be the last time I saw my baby alive.

After the operation, the surgeon came down to the waiting area to talk to us. He said that when Kylie was being transferred from the operating room to the neonatal intensive care unit, one of the chest tubes had fallen on her heart, compressing a coronary artery and interrupting blood flow to a portion of the heart for a short period. He was unsure if Kylie's brain was ever without blood flow. He added that Kylie was resting comfortably and had been put on a revolutionary heart-lung bypass machine known as ECMO (Extra Corporeal Membrane Oxygenation).

The sight of our baby girl with multiple tubes in her neck, deathly still and swollen, was more than I could bear. I sobbed to anyone who could hear, "Oh, Lord, please save our little girl. Help!"

Wednesday, February 19: Three nurses cared for Kylie at all times. I read to her and sang songs that I recorded on tape for the nurses to play at night when I wasn't there. Maybe hearing Mommy's voice would sooth and comfort her.

After three days, Kylie came off the ECMO machine but was still less than stable. Her ailments included a rapid heartbeat and low blood pressure for the next week. The roller-coaster ride of recovery continued for eight days until doctors were able to close her chest, but hospitalization would be required for several more weeks.

When Kylie's older brother, Jarrett, was finally allowed to visit, they covered the baby with a blanket so Jarrett would only see her face. "She has a mustache!" he told his dad, mistakenly identifying the tubes and bandages on her little face. The doctor told Jesse that their love and support for Kylie was the most important thing they could do. "Just love her," he said. Fortunately, that was easy to do.

Two-and-a-half weeks after surgery, Kylie Nicole went home to her big brother and a welcoming family who had been praying for this moment since her birth. "She's our little miracle," said Jesse.

A Big Story

Most babies don't end up as feature stories in the local newspaper, but Kylie Wright was different. On the front page of the *San Diego Union-Tribune,* the caption under a half-page picture of twenty-month-old Kylie Wright and her mom read: "Prayers Come True: When Kylie Wright was born with heart problems, her mother, Jesse, put her faith in God and modern medicine. Her prayers were answered because Kylie is a happy, healthy baby girl . . . ."

The touching story accompanying the photo related how medical advancements, a tough little girl, and prayerful parents were all working together to save the baby's life.

At twenty months, Kylie took her first steps. "Up tall, Kylie," her therapist would encourage. Once her little legs grew stronger, there was no stopping the little dynamo. Although she was slow to reach some of the milestones of babyhood, it was only a matter of time until Kylie was exceeding her peers in physical and mental development.

The Wright home normalized, as routine visits to the cardiologist were required only on an annual basis. "I wouldn't suggest running marathons," the doctor advised, "but this little gal is progressing normally. I look forward to seeing her in a year. No restrictions."

A Friend to Everyone

Kylie was six years old—an outgoing, soft hearted, fun-loving little girl. In contrast, brother Jarrett was quiet and reserved. Kylie became her brother's mouthpiece. If he needed something, she was there to see he got it. When he was discouraged, she was his champion. In exchange, Jarrett took care of his sister, always making sure everything was "great" with Kylie. Their bond had been sealed from the day Baby Kylie came home from the hospital.

Kylie was a friend to everyone, especially those who really needed a friend. And Kylie *really* loved Jesus. She wanted to make sure that all the people she loved were going to heaven.

One day, she met the San Diego Chargers running back LaDainian Tomlinson, who was in the prime of his career. While everyone else asked him questions about football and if the Chargers were going to the Super Bowl, the first question Kylie asked him was, "Are you a Christian?"

The famous running back smiled at her and said, "Yes, I am." That was the kind of precious, special little girl she was.

Just days before Kylie's tenth birthday, Jesse told Kylie she was going to have a baby brother. While a bit disappointed "her" baby wasn't going to be a girl, she was delighted to have the honor of announcing the new family member at her birthday party. After some consideration, Kylie told her mom she was glad the baby would be a boy so that she could be the only girl in the family.

Baby Kendrick stole Kylie's heart. From their first meeting in the hospital, Kylie found it difficult to share her little brother. When Kendrick was just ten months old, Kylie suggested that he should go to school with her so she might show him to all her friends and teachers. This little miracle of life followed Kylie around, climbing up on the piano bench to be near her when she practiced or when she played her grandpa's favorite piece, "Für Elise," at her Christmas recital. The Wright family was knit together in mutual love.

By sixth grade, Kylie was cleared to be a cheerleader, where her gorgeous smile captured the hearts of those she led in cheers.

Everything seemed normal for this child who had had such a frightful beginning to her life.

Gifts for the Family

It was sixth grade graduation time. Junior high school was ahead of her, and Kylie, still a bit of a tomboy, looked forward to a summer of swimming and outdoor fun before entering the next phase of her education.

One day, Kylie went shopping with her grandmother. Typical of her giving nature, Kylie bought gifts for her family: a Barry Manilow CD for her mom; a Snickers bar for her dad; and T-shirts for her brothers. Kylie and her grandmother stopped by her parents' house to show her folks the clothes they had bought and to present them with their gifts.

Later that day, a violent earthquake shook Southern California. By this time, Kylie and Jarrett were at their grandparents' home and were fine. When her mother called to check on her, Kylie told her that her grandpa was taking them out to dinner, although that was news to Jesse. Sure enough, they did go out to dinner, and upon their return, Kylie called Jesse and left a voicemail, telling her mom she loved her—something she ordinarily didn't do.

After dinner, the evening was still warm. Kylie and Jarrett asked if they could swim in the backyard pool as a "special treat." The grandparents said fine.

The two children frolicked in the water for a while, and then Kylie climbed out of the pool to take a break. Suddenly, she collapsed onto a chaise lounge—as if she had been pulled from the pool unconscious.

Jarrett screamed. His grandmother, who was keeping an eye on the children, rushed to Kylie's side.

"Go get Grandpa!" she yelled.

Jarrett sprinted into the home while she held Kyle, praying for her life. She felt a whoosh of wind, as gentle as an angel's wing, blow across her face. She distinctly heard a voice say, *She's not going to make it.* Angered, she looked around to see who would make such a devastating comment. She and Kylie were alone in the yard.

Her husband, a medical doctor, came running out, quickly assessed the situation, and started CPR. Meanwhile, Jarrett ran back into the house and called his mother.

"Kylie's not breathing," he said, his voice shaking. "Gramma's trying to help her!"

"Call 911 right now!" Jesse cried back into the phone.

Paramedics arrived quickly and made several attempts to shock Kylie's heart. They succeeded in stimulating a faint beat. Kylie was rushed to Palomar Hospital, where the family converged upon the Intensive Care Unit. While doctors worked on her, arrangements were made to have Life Flight transport her to Rady Children's Hospital fifteen miles to the south.

"Who's the most emotionally stable parent?" one of the paramedics asked.

"That would be me!" Jesse exclaimed, feeling anything but stable. Jesse climbed into the 'copter for the short ride to Children's Hospital.

Once there, a CAT scan and MRIs were performed. For six days, Kylie, unconscious, clung to life. Jesse, Kent, and Jarrett held her, talked to her, and said their goodbyes. Her precious little life seemed to be receding from her body. When Kylie took her last breath, Jesse knew Kylie was in heaven.

At that instant, a poignant Bible verse crossed Jesse's mind—something about "soaring on wings like eagles," she thought. In her mind's eye, she saw Kylie soaring to her eternal home at that very moment.

That night Jesse located the verse that immediately touched her heart.

But those who hope in the Lord will renew their strength. They will soar on wings like eagles; they will run and not grow weary, they will walk and not be faint.

—Isaiah 40:31 (NIV)

How comforting it was to think of Kylie running and not fainting. Jesse asked for "hope in the Lord" and a "renewed strength" as she wept for the void in their lives that would never be filled. For twelve years, five months, and five days, Kylie was the light of their lives.

More Comfort Is Needed

Just seven weeks after Kylie's services, a girlfriend called Jesse and asked if she could come over and talk. Expecting words of comfort, Jesse was surprised to hear her girlfriend bring up the name of a family whose son had been born with the same heart defect as her daughter. At that moment, fifteen-year-old Graham lay unconscious in a hospital bed, his parents holding onto hope for his recovery.

"What do you want me to do about this?" Jesse asked her friend.

"Nothing," she replied. "I just wanted to tell you so you are aware."

When Jesse returned home, she sat on a couch in her living room. "Lord, what do you expect me to do about this?" she prayed. Her grief was still raw. She had barely been able to deal with Kylie's clothes and belongings. How could she reach out to someone else?

"For I know the plans I have for you, plans to prosper you and not to harm you, plans to give you a hope and a future."

She knew that verse: Jeremiah 29:11 (NIV). God had plans for her, possibly to reach out to this family.

When Jesse entered the hospital waiting room, she was recognized by the friends and family gathered there for support. Graham's mother actually thought Kylie had recovered and was at home, but many knew of her recent loss. Jesse was struck with the knowledge that she did not represent hope for this family, but she still wanted to speak gently to the parents and family members.

"I have come to bring hope for your son," Jesse said. "We don't know the outcome, but we can hope and pray. I am here to help in any way I can." The mothers inside the waiting room embraced and huddled together to discuss the situation.

Jesse made it a point to be with Graham's family every day, praying, encouraging, and doing errands that needed to be done. The families were walking the journey together. Jesse realized how blessed she was and how much stronger she had become by reaching out to help another family.

Graham passed away two months to the day after Kylie had died. Together, the two families gained strength and courage to face the days without their children. Graham's younger sister, Piper, and Jarrett talked and walked together, inspiring a friendship that continues today.

As for Jesse, faith in God's strength, not her own, allowed her to walk alongside another and in so doing, Jesse was filled with the compassion needed to help and support this family. Her daughter's legacy inspired Jesse to touch the lives of others who find themselves in a valley of despair.

Again, a verse from Jesse's Bible entered her mind, confirming the loss of Kylie would not consume her life, but develop in her an understanding and compassion for others who are suffering a loss.

She hung on to this verse:

Because of the Lord's great love, we are not consumed,
for his compassions never fail.

—Lamentations 3:22

The Encouraging Dream

A year or so after Kylie's death, God blessed Jesse with a unique experience.

One night, exhausted, she went to bed early, awaking in the morning feeling exceptionally refreshed. Her eyes widened as her dream from this restful night came back to her memory. In her dream, the doorbell rang. Jesse opened the door, and there in her dream was Kylie. She heard the words of the Lord saying, *Since I took Kylie so suddenly, I'm going to give you all one last day with her.*

What a day it was. Jesse listened while Kylie told the family about heaven. They all went swimming together, one of Kylie's favorite things to do. They played a fun board game and then Kylie made a beeline for the family piano, where she played Grandpa's favorite piece for the whole family.

They laughed. They hugged. It was one of those memorable, perfect days where Jesse felt the happiest she'd been since her daughter's death. At the end of the day, after a family barbecue, Kylie turned to say goodbye. She hugged her mom, saying, "I'm okay. I'm happy." And then she winked and was gone.

This time around, Jesse felt no sadness. She was joyful for the time they had spent together in her dream. Even now, Jesse believes God gave her that perfect day with Kylie so that her last memory was not a lifeless form but one of His precious child.

Jesse continues to be amazed at how God filled the void left by Kylie's absence. Kylie's life has been honored through Jesse's reaching out to people whose lives are brought down by their circumstances, a testimony to God's provision and a means of paying life's blessings forward.

Thoughts to Ponder

- Use a journal to describe a favorite day with your child. Take time to go back to the description and add more detail.

- List the people you know who are in need of a helping hand. What one thing could you do to help their situation?

- Call a friend today and ask her to walk with you or have lunch or come over for a cup of coffee. Your friends want to be near you. Include them in your journey; they will be an added comfort in your loss.

A Closer Look: Jesse Wright

As Jesse looks back at the years leading up to the death of her precious daughter, she sees that while she thought she was simply living her life, God was actually placing people and circumstances in her path that would help her through her devastating loss as well as allow her to be used to help others.

Jesse has since become a Court Appointed Special Advocate for the foster youth of San Diego. In addition, her involvement with Catering for Christ gives her the opportunity to minister to families who have experienced a tragic loss and literally sustain them with a hearty meal. Her legacy to Kylie is to carry the joy of her daughter to others and, in so doing, keep Kylie's memory close to her heart.

Her son, Jarrett, has recently graduated from Biola University in Los Angeles. The loss of his sister has given him a tender heart toward those in need. Kendrick, now nine, not only looks like Kylie but also shares her mannerisms and endearing smile.

Kent has drawn closer to his family and friends, recognizing that one's world can change forever in the blink of an eye. Today, he's touching people for Jesus now that his faith has been renewed.

3

Use Us Lord!

An Avoidable Stillbirth Brings Forth a Prayer

"We're expecting!"

This emotionally packed statement announcing a new life is usually followed by squeals of excitement and joyous hugs. The miracle of birth is a marvel that can multiply the love between a husband and wife with the addition of a new baby.

Nine months of preparation allow time for parents to reorganize their lives, debate the most appropriate name for their little girl or boy, paint a nursery, and watch a profoundly swelling belly forecast the approaching arrival of their precious baby. Evolving within is the miraculous dividing of two cells into a beautiful human form, with all the moving parts necessary to function upon delivery. Expectations are for a perfect child, anticipating a lifetime with this very special gift.

* * *

Three years after Sherry and Steve Hougard married, they proclaimed these words of expectation. Their relationship had started when they met at a dinner party. Steve was conversing with one of Sherry's good friends when she naturally joined in their conversation. He was taken with her frank and perky spirit that came through that night. They spent the rest of the evening talking and continued getting to know each other on the phone over the course of the next week.

Sherry had been raised by nurturing Christian parents, growing up with a practical, outspoken faith in the God she knew personally. At an early age, she would talk to God about what was right and wrong and seek His direction. Prayer was a conversation that went on all day. She developed strong opinions, an exceptional talent for organizing everything and everyone, and an eye for simple beauty, reflected in her appearance and her heart.

Steve, on the other hand, had quit going to church as soon as he was old enough and his mom couldn't make him go. As his relationship with Sherry became more serious, though, Steve found himself desiring the same strong faith he saw in Sherry's life. Within a few months of their meeting, he and Sherry got down on their knees in his living room, where he gave his life to the Lord and prayed that their lives together would be a witness to their mutual faith.

Complications or Indigestion?

Preparation was Sherry's middle name. Having announced to family and friends the good news of her pregnancy, she went to work decorating the nursery and supplying it with all the accoutrements for the care and feeding of their baby. Friends showered the couple with gifts and waited to hear that Baby Hougard had arrived.

Three weeks prior to her due date, Sherry began feeling light headed, alternating with a flushed warmth and a rapid heartbeat. Sharp pains banded around her upper abdomen. When she called her doctor, he suggested it was indigestion and that she be more careful about what she ate and get more rest.

But Sherry knew something was wrong. Finally, she insisted on being seen by a doctor who immediately rushed her to the hospital. Sherry was experiencing a rare form of toxemia called HELLP syndrome, a pregnancy-induced hypertension that, if misdiagnosed, can cause liver failure and loss of both the mother and child's life.

Immediately, an emergency Caesarian section was performed, and their little baby girl—whom they named Madison—was lifted out of the womb to safety while Sherry's condition was successfully treated. Young and healthy, Sherry recovered her strength and determined to put aside her resentment toward the doctors who failed to hear her earnest concerns. As far as the doctors and patient knew, her physical healing was complete.

Steve and Sherry began their parenting journey with a deep gratitude for this blessing and were keenly mindful that walking by faith holds no guarantee of a trouble-free life. They memorized the verse John 16:33 (NIV): "I have told you these things, so that in me you may have peace. In this world you will have trouble. But take heart! I have overcome the world."

Unmet Expectations

Working together, Sherry and Steve designed and built a new home for their growing family. Their second child was due shortly, and three-year-old Madison helped with the preparations. Their friendship circle included a dozen young couples who were also awaiting the birth of their babies, inspiring numerous showers with animated conversations about childbirth and child-rearing. Twelve babies were due within a two-month period.

The day before her due date, Sherry again suspected complications. She called the hospital to request a stress test, but the neonatal nurse's station didn't call back. Once again, sharp pains came from the upper portion of her abdomen. Her condition was turning serious. Steven and Sherry prayed together as they sped to the hospital, putting their baby's health in God's hands. Sherry felt a sharp tear from within her uterus as they pulled into the emergency area, and she was whisked into delivery. By the time she was hooked up to the various monitoring devices, the faint heartbeat had stopped.

From deep within Sherry, a wail of despair broke through her clenched teeth. "Are you sure we can't save her?" she cried out. They had been told that they were expecting a girl.

Steve held her hand in his as tears streamed down their faces. The pain of delivering a stillborn child was magnified by the heart-wrenching awareness of their loss. Beautiful and perfectly formed, their little girl was placed in Sherry's arms as Steve knelt by her bed and prayed out loud to the God they both loved, "Lord, make us usable in this loss. Together we pray to be a testimony to Your power and grace. Use us, Lord, as a witness to others. Thy will be done, here on earth, as it is in Your Heavenly place."

The lowest moment of their lives was lifted up and released like a butterfly flying from the cocoon. Their daughter, whom they named Paige, was now in heaven.

Is There Any Comfort?

From the moment of that prayer, Sherry and Steve were given the gift of purpose—the knowledge that what they did with their experience could change others' lives. Sherry was aware of a young nurse in training who appeared overwhelmed by the ordeal and labor Sherry had gone through while delivering a baby whose heart had stopped beating.

When Sherry and Steve prayed that day, the young nurse stood in awe as she observed God's presence in their hearts; a peace that she struggled to understand. Yes, there were tears—lots of tears for the letting go of expectations and anticipation of life. The process of grieving was unfolding, but they were holding onto the promises and hope of being used. Sherry began to hum and then sang a song from her Sunday school days with the lyric, "The Lord is my Shepherd, I shall not want . . . ."

Sherry held the hand of the young nurse and prayed for her to see God's promise of comfort to those who enter the valley of the shadow of death.

Awkward Moments

A week after Sherry left the hospital, she and four-year-old Madison were standing in a check-out line at Costco behind a new mother comforting her crying baby. Sherry's emotions were on edge, heightened by all the hormonal changes her body was experiencing. Tears sprung to her eyes as she turned away from the cooing mother. Madison took in the scene and reached out for her mother's hand.

"Mom," the preschooler said, "It's okay. We'll see Paige in heaven."

A smile spread across Sherry's face. She hugged her daughter and said, "You're so right, honey! Thank you for reminding me." At that moment, Sherry determined to double her focus on Madison and the pleasure she brought to their family. Being an attentive mom for Madison would fill the void and deflect the pain that seemed to continually resurface, she thought.

One by one, the twelve other families delivered their healthy babies. While Sherry and Steve rejoiced with their friends, there was a gnawing resentment that filled Sherry as she listened to the conversations about the stages and pleasures of their new additions. For weeks she fought the bitterness that came with comparisons like:

- *Their child is perfect, while mine is gone from my sight.*

- *Their nursery smells of lotion and powder, while mine is empty and silent.*

- *Their parenting brings them joy, while I fight to break through the sadness each day.*

When these unwanted feelings of resentment would start to build, Sherry would search her Bible for a psalm to help her praise God for these families and for her personal blessings, which she had to admit were many. She made the choice to awaken every morning thanking God for her life. She learned a heart filled with gratitude had little room for bitterness.

Some friends avoided contact with Sherry, not knowing how to handle their good fortune in light of her loss. Others who were not aware of what had happened would see Sherry and say, "Oh! You've had the baby. How's it going?" Embarrassment and awkward exchanges would follow. Sherry quickly came to the realization that it was part of her purpose to deal with this discomfort in a manner that put well-meaning friends and acquaintances at ease.

The grieving process, she learned, had no timeframe. Steve and Sherry committed to studying God's Word for their strength and joy in time of sorrow. She would awaken at 2 a.m. and let the verses speak to her when she felt life was unraveling. Slowly the fog of despair began to lift, and the couple's hearts began to feel the comfort they were claiming. The sense of drowning in their sorrow gradually gave way to a sense of resurfacing, coming up for air, and reestablishing the routines of daily life.

Sherry soon discovered she was again pregnant with a new life. Since she had delivered Paige naturally, though she did not live, her doctor predicted a natural childbirth, not a Caesarian section. "No reason not to," her ob-gyn concluded.

A Sudden Change

The doctors' relaxed attitude troubled Sherry. When her blood pressure began to rise in the seventh month, she insisted on being taken to the hospital for monitoring.

On May 21, a year and a day after Paige's death, five-year-old Madison came with her father to visit her mother. The kindergartner looked very serious as she said, "Mom, cut this baby out. I can't lose another baby."

Hearing her daughter say that was like a weight was lifted from Sherry's mind. She had struggled with the doctor's determination to let the baby be delivered naturally. She immediately asked the nurse to contact her doctor. When the physician arrived, she asked her to please deliver the baby as soon as it was safe to do a Caesarian birth. She made the request with such determination that the doctor wrote on her chart *possible Caesarian section*. When Sherry's blood pressure raced higher and the bands of pain under her ribs increased, the decision was made to perform a C-section. Even though Sherry was not full-term at thirty-six weeks, their son, Nate, was born healthy and ready to fill the nursery with his presence.

Two years later, when a fourth pregnancy was underway, precautions were in place and plans made for this child to be delivered by Caesarian about a month prior to the due date. Baby daughter Shayne was born safely, and the family once again felt a joyous relief.

Healing Is Not Forgetting

The Hougard family of five continues to purposefully remember Paige's birth. Each year on Paige's birth date, the family chooses a needy recipient to receive an anonymous gift in her honor. Several years ago they searched the website for World Vision, a Christian relief organization where families can sponsor children in poor countries, including children with special needs. In searching the website, they came upon a girl born on the exact day and year as Paige! Celebrating this child's life with their financial contributions kept alive their purpose of "Use us, Lord!"

"We were never given the promise that all things on this earth would end well," Sherry reflected. "Life at any point is fragile. Steve and I have learned to hold loosely those who we love but do everything we can to make sure they are firmly held in God's hands. He never assured us that our walk would be along an easy path here on earth. In fact, He proclaims we will have troubles in John 16:33. But He did promise that He would walk through them with us."

Sherry's testimony of healing continues today. In dealing with some personal health issues, Sherry recognized her need to frankly admit her feelings of disappointment and honestly share the pain of losing a child at birth. In attempting to demonstrate God's strength in her life, she had always held back the tears and confessions of doubt. But His peace and comfort were magnified when her prayers were spoken with the frankness with which she lifted her concerns to the Lord as a teenager.

She wasn't afraid to ask "Why did this happen, Lord?" or "Where is Your power in the loss of life here on earth?" Asking God questions, even in despair, allowed for the emotional and physical healing she would not have known from simply leaning on her own strength. "I fully have come to understand the peace that passes all understanding," she said. "His Word is alive, and it spoke peace to me when I was honest with Him in my doubting moments. God is faithful to His Word and He continues to show me His ways in my life."

Thoughts to Ponder

- Resentment and bitterness hinder our path of healing. Daily lifting up the negative emotions and consciously focusing on blessings in the midst of our deep loss will bring light into the darkness of despair. Each day write one thing for which you are thankful. Write these blessings on your calendar for the entire month.

- When you are ready, write a prayer as a *thank you* note to God for the memories you treasure of your child. Share it with your spouse or a friend.

- Find a way to honor your children on either their birth date or the day of their death. Seek out projects where your talent might be used. In helping others, you will be lifted up.

About the Mother: Sherry Hougard

Sherry is a native Californian, one of the first babies born at Scripps Memorial Hospital in La Jolla, California. Her son Nate and daughter Shayne were born at the same hospital.

For the past several years, Sherry has been involved with a group called *Moms in Prayer*, a gathering of mothers with school-aged children who support each other in prayer. Each year Sherry organizes a mothers' retreat entitled Random Moms' Retreat due to the arbitrary way in which mothers might find themselves attending the annual gathering. Steve commits himself to leading a weekly men's Bible study while continuing to develop his home loan business.

These days, the Hougards' home is filled with the sounds of children. Madison is sixteen, Nate is eleven, and Shayne is nine. Sherry and Steve recently celebrated nineteen years of marriage. Remembering Paige and what she meant to them remains a focal part of their family values.

Author's Note

Two years after the Hougards' loss of Paige, my stepson Jason's wife, Tina, delivered a full-term, stillborn baby boy named Ari. Tina had experienced the same band of abdominal pains a few days prior to the due date of this baby, her third child. A placental abruption had occurred. Tina, like Sherry, knew during her labor and delivery that she was delivering a baby who had already gone to heaven.

Sherry was the first person we called for support and encouragement for Tina. The two mothers shared their common sorrow and their struggles, declaring through it all that they were placing their trust and love in the Lord for His provision. Sherry concluded that her loss of Paige allowed God to use her to help Tina and Jason. In reaching out, Sherry herself was strengthened. In giving, she was blessed.

Tina and Jason have since given us two more healthy, beautiful grandsons. When asked about his family, their oldest son Benjamin always answers that he has four brothers, but that baby brother Ari is already in heaven.

4

Dreams for a Family

Moving Beyond Guilt After Multiple Miscarriages

Miscarriage.

When the word is applied to the premature death of a baby, a child inside the womb, mothers agonize as to what they could have done differently. Did they disrupt the natural process? If not, then why did their baby die?

In this compelling chapter, Julie Bendinelli shares her experience of multiple miscarriages, which ultimately led to an intimate understanding of God's incredible power to wipe away not only the tears but also the plaguing sense of guilt.

* * *

Tom and Julie Bendinelli were happily married for two years before their first baby was conceived. Both incredibly fit and healthy, they were surprised it took so long for their dream to come true—to become parents.

Julie's body adjusted to the presence of a baby in her womb. Morning sickness passed, and then all her hormones kicked into gear. She actually had breasts; a real treat for this slim and trim mother-to-be. Their marriage took on a new excitement as Tom and Julie discussed names, what color to paint the nursery, and opening a savings account to fund college.

Every conversation seemed to center around the budding

child they had created. Tom and Julie were filled with joy and expectation, but they decided to wait until their traditional Christmas gathering a couple of months later to announce the news. What a celebration that would be for the extended family!

News of Julie's pregnancy was greeted with excitement around the Christmas tree, as they expected. Just four days after Christmas, Julie and Tom went in for the first ultrasound to check on the fetal growth as well as to determine if they were having a baby boy or girl. As Julie lay watching the monitor, she could tell the doctor was taking longer than expected to report the results. There was absolute silence as the scope continued back and forth across her pelvis.

"Julie, Tom," the doctor said quietly, "I think we've lost this little one. There's no heartbeat."

The room spun for Julie. *This can't be possible*, she thought frantically.

Panic rose in her face. "Oh, no!" she sobbed. "Can you keep checking?"

The doctor passed the scope over her skin and peered for a long time at the monitor. Then he shook his head. "Julie, we need to schedule you for a D&C, a dilation and curettage."

"Is that like an abortion?" Julie whispered.

"Yes. It's the same procedure," he responded.

"That's out of the question." She sat up and faced the doctor. "I refuse."

The doctor explained to Julie and Tom that without the procedure, they would have to endure the time it took the body to naturally expel the baby. There would be cramping and possibly much bleeding. Julie emphatically insisted she did not feel comfortable having the D&C procedure. The two quietly left the office for an unbearably silent, tearful ride to their home.

Just a few hours earlier, their lives had been filled with joy and expectation. Now they headed down a path filled with grief.

Tom sought to console Julie. His approach was more logical, saying sometimes these things happen in a pregnancy and it wasn't their time yet. His soothing words were met with more tears, however.

"Why wasn't it the right time?" she asked. "What did I do wrong? Why can't I have my baby alive inside me now?"

Tom didn't have any answers. Two days later, the cramping and blood flow began. Julie's sadness was overwhelming as her body naturally released her baby.

Looking Ahead

New Year's Eve was a somber night for the two of them, but Tom encouraged Julie to look to the coming year with hope and anticipation. "This was our first baby. There will be many more in our future. I know it," he said. Tom pulled her close, and then the two of them prayed for a year unlike the one that just passed. They prayed that they would have a year where they would welcome a child into their family.

Tom had been the one to tell the family and a few of their friends that Julie had lost the child. Julie couldn't face them. Every morning she prayed for the strength to just get out of bed. Having never known another woman who had experienced her loss, she had no one to turn to except her journal. Two and three times a day, she entered her deepest feelings of failure.

"Will I ever become a mother? "she questioned. "Where was the God I have grown up loving and trusting?" Honest emotions spilled out onto the pages, releasing pent-up thoughts and searing observations about what the miscarriage meant to her.

Tom, along with friends and family, plied her with words of encouragement. Many were a variation of the same theme: *This was just the first time. You can have many more children.*

Those words provided no comfort for the pain that surrounded her after creating a baby and then not having that child to hold, nurture, and love. Sure, there might be more children, maybe, but what about this baby?

Her depression isolated her from others who did not understand what she was going through. She craved sitting down with someone who could listen to her feelings, someone who had walked in her shoes and had survived a loss similar to hers. She felt judged for her depressed state, for not being more resilient.

Lastly, Julie resented the shallow encouragement from others to leave the past behind. *What's done is done*, she heard well-meaning folks say. *You have to move on.*

What did they know? Their children were alive. Her baby had died inside her body.

In her heart, Julie believed she was destined to become a mom. She loved babies and children of all ages. In the past, their dolls and toys would bring a smile to her face as she would get down on the floor to share make-believe adventures with cute toddlers.

At the same time, she felt God was clearly speaking through her loss, that she needed to be patient. Things could take a while. Her doctor deemed their loss as an "early miscarriage"—one experienced in the first trimester of a pregnancy. There was no reason that she and Tom could not to look forward to a successful full-term pregnancy. Six months after the miscarriage, Julie was given the green light to try again.

Putting their experience in God's hands, Julie became pregnant ten months after her miscarriage. Determined not to lose this baby, she gave up caffeine, stopped drinking anything with artificial sweeteners, and considered becoming a vegetarian. She longed for someone to explain to her why her baby died and how she might have been at fault. Was it the pesticides from visiting her father's farm? If she knew what caused the loss, then Julie would feel more in control of this next pregnancy.

This time around, the ultrasound proved this baby to be a little girl. They decided they would name her Taylor. Meanwhile, the pregnancy progressed well. As they entered the fifth month, though, the doctor noticed that the baby was not growing at the normal rate. Typically ultrasounds are performed in the first and last trimester, but the doctor was concerned that the baby might not be positioned right or that the heart was not forming correctly. Another ultrasound was scheduled.

The ultrasound at twenty weeks showed that the baby wasn't developing in size as expected.

"Julie," the doctor quietly spoke. "We need to do an amniocentesis. Your baby could have Down syndrome."

"NO!" Julie replied spontaneously. "If she does, I don't want to know. We will accept Taylor just as she is!"

Tom looked at Julie with a deep sadness in his eyes. "Julie," he said as he took her hand, "We just need to be prepared. I need to be prepared."

The doctor left them alone in the examination room. Tom shook his head. "Julie, I don't know if I have it in me to raise a Down syndrome child. I'm just being honest with you. Please, don't be angry with me, but I'm scared. Scared of what this means to our lives."

Julie was silent. She thought for a moment, saying a silent prayer within herself before speaking. "Tom, I truly respect what you are saying, but understand this; I will raise Taylor with or without you by my side."

The Waiting

The amniocentesis was performed, but it would be ten days before the results could be analyzed. While Julie had made it clear that she didn't want to know the test results, she changed her mind after discussing the matter with Tom. Whatever the result, Julie said, she was still having the baby.

She and Tom were at the movies when she saw a call coming through from her doctor. She left the theater to take the call.

Her heart was in her throat as she listened. "The results do not indicate Down syndrome," the doctor began, "but there are further complications. The heart has not formed properly, but our goal now is to keep this baby inside the womb for as long as possible so that she can develop her lungs long enough to survive on the outside. Then we will determine what we need to do for her heart."

A plan was prepared for Taylor's birth, with the goal to deliver the child naturally. A neonatal specialist was familiarized with the baby's condition. As her due date of August 7 drew closer, the doctor insisted upon a C-section as soon as she went into labor. Julie prayed Taylor would remain protected within her as long as possible.

On the Fourth of July, though, early fireworks happened. The placenta lining abruptly separated from the uterus, causing pain and bleeding as well as an immediate threat to both mother and baby. Julie was rushed to the hospital where a C-section was performed to save the baby. Little Taylor was delivered at four pounds, six ounces, and she was briefly placed in Julie's arms to admire and pray a silent prayer for her well-being. Then the infant was rushed to the neonatal ICU, where specialists monitored her continually. The hope was to get through at least another month so that her lungs could further develop before performing the necessary heart surgery.

Because of the heart defect, Taylor's health was deteriorating. Nine days after her birth, the decision was made to do open heart surgery immediately. Julie and Tom endured the longest day of their lives. After six hours, the doctors reported they were able to make all the necessary repairs. Now it was up to Taylor.

Inside the neonatal unit, she was kept on machines sustaining her breathing and body temperature. Julie and Tom were there every day, only returning home in the evening to sleep. They saw other babies joining Taylor in the battle for life.

Taylor continued to rely on the machines, but she was unable to sustain herself without the pumps and ventilators. Julie prayed with confidence that God wouldn't take this baby from them. *Don't doubt this,* she scolded herself. *We are taking this baby home with us!*

And then Taylor took her last breath.

The only way Julie could rationalize what happened is that God had left her. The amazing God of the Universe who could do anything had left her in the lurch. Why didn't God use His power to heal Taylor? Why did He just let it . . . happen?

A nurse wrapped Taylor in a pink blanket for Julie to hold. She still looked so perfect, so precious, like a peaceful, sleeping baby. A triage nurse took a photo of Julie with Taylor, but Julie never asked for a copy. The image she wanted in her mind was of her daughter alive, not dead.

The Empty Nursery

Julie and Tom returned home to an empty house, where Taylor's room was ready with handmade curtains, comforter, and bumper pads all made from the same smokey blue fabric. The chair-rail border around the room separated the smokey blue solid bottom from the top, which had little white polka dots that had been lovingly applied on the blue fabric by Julie. Shower gifts of adorable little pajamas, lacy pink outfits, and baby toys were tucked away on shelves and in drawers.

Julie's sister-in-law was expecting her third child—a third daughter—at the same time. Julie couldn't endure attending her shower, but she did visit Tom's sister after Samantha was born. How hard was it for her to hold that precious healthy baby, but Julie knew in her heart, below the deep grief, that a special bond was formed that day.

Still, every day held its difficulties. One night, in trying to console Julie, Tom said, "Well, you did get to hold her!" Julie knew he meant those words to be a salve for her pain, but there were not words or memories that could cushion the blow of losing Taylor.

A few days later, a dear friend came to the door one morning with an interesting proposition.

"Julie," she said, "I'm here to pray with you and then help you get your butt out of bed!"

Next, her friend proceeded to pack up all the shower gifts so that they could be sent back. Then Julie cleaned up her desk and tossed out handfuls of sympathy cards, which she had come to loath.

"I *hate* sympathy cards," Julie told her friend. "They say terrible things that people repeat. Who writes those cards? Why can't people just send a personal note written from their heart? I know there are no words to take away this pain, but at least people could just say they care! I guess there's no instruction book for how to get through the death of your child!"

Of all her eighteen cousins, she was the first to experience the death of a child, not once, but twice. Up until that day, no one denied her the right to grieve. But her insistent friend, she recognized, was God's hand reaching out to touch her life.

At one level, Julie understood that life had to go on. She worked in the pharmaceutical industry in sales, but most of her work was done in the field. She rotated through five different outside offices where the staff was not familiar with how Julie's pregnancies ended.

Julie was allowed extra time off to regain her strength and courage to get back to the outside world. In late September, two months after the death of Taylor, she checked in at the first of five offices to let everyone know she would be starting back to work soon.

"Oh!" exclaimed the receptionist, "you had your baby!"

Julie was caught off guard. She held her breath for a moment to collect her composure. Then she quickly explained her baby had died and she walked hurriedly into the interior offices.

By the third office visit, she lost it. She drove home barely able to drive, unstoppable tears flowing down her cheeks. Julie knew she would not be able to face everyone with an explanation of her loss, so she and Tom printed cards announcing both Taylor's birth and death dates. After placing the cards in the mail, Julie took another month off of work.

A Different Way to Grieve

Julie would not let Tom dismantle the crib. She found herself dwelling in self-pity, her depression tying her to the painful past. Tom found other things to focus on. He mentally moved on more quickly than she. Julie found it endearing that Tom kept the shirt he was wearing on the day of Taylor's death. He never wore it again, but the smell of their little baby lingered for some time. The polo shirt was neatly folded in a drawer in Taylor's memory.

One morning, Julie awoke brightly—as if a cloud had lifted from her mind. She realized she *had* been a mom—if only for a few short days. She was blessed to hold Taylor. She looked at the announcement cards they had sent out and realized how they were acknowledging her life and her name. The pain of loss was still apparent in her heart, but she left her bed that morning determined to move forward. She went into the kitchen and snuggled into Tom's arms, bringing a smile of hopefulness to his face. Without speaking, he could feel the change in Julie's composure. They would never forget Taylor but they had each other and, in that moment, a mutual agreement to look to their future.

When Christmas rolled around, Julie had returned to work but there was greater news to share with the family: she was pregnant again. Everyone was overjoyed, but by Valentine's Day, Julie felt something was wrong.

Panic rising, she called the doctor and was told they had no openings. "You will just have to wait until tomorrow," the receptionist responded.

Julie hung up the phone and fell apart, crying uncontrollably.

"Just go in!" Tom told her. He was leaving town that afternoon on a business trip.

It was getting late, so Julie decided to go to the obstetrics office without an appointment. When she finally got to see her doctor, he listened for a heartbeat—and immediately called paramedics to take her to the emergency room.

Julie, terribly worried, called Tom and caught him at the airport just before he was to board the plane.

"I'm coming, Julie!" he said after hearing the news. By the time Tom arrived at the hospital, Julie was told that she was carrying a baby girl whose heart must have stopped beating about a week or so prior. The news was devastating.

Once again, Julie refused the D&C procedure. After a week of slow dilation, labor began and once again, her body naturally released her baby.

Julie was inconsolable. She-hadn't had time to even think about naming her baby, nor did Julie have the strength to give any recognition to the tiny life that had passed away. An autopsy showed the heart had not developed properly, a mirror image of Taylor's problems. The baby also had a cleft palate with the center of her mouth not formed.

"Why is this happening to me?" she asked God. "Why can't I be a mother like every other woman I know? I'm such a failure."

This time around, Julie's response to her loss was drastically different from her previous two occasions. Taylor's death had been intolerable. The room had been prepared for Taylor, the clothes were in place, and her name was a reality in their hearts and minds. To have held in her arms their beautifully formed baby and then to let her go was the worst of all losses for Julie.

This time around, Julie went on a mission. She found a genetic counselor who performed a few tests. The results indicated Julie had a 50/50 chance of delivering a baby with serious health conditions. Those were terrible genetic odds. Julie was counseled to apply for adoption and not try again to become pregnant.

An Attitude of Perseverance

Julie did not accept the prognosis. She felt like the Lord was telling her to continue trusting in Him. She and Tom tried again.

Julie researched and found a woman doctor who partnered with Julie to bring about a successful pregnancy. Every week on her lunch break, the doctor would monitor the growing baby's heartbeat. After each visit, Julie would write in her prayer journal a conversational letter of encouragement to her baby.

"Dear Baby," she wrote, "I heard your heartbeat today. I know you are developing according to God's plan for you to join our family."

Four weeks prior to the due date, her doctor determined that the birth should be induced. Twenty-three-and-a-half hours of labor produced a son that Tom and Julie named Dominic. This baby showed signs of non life-threatening pulmonary stenosis as well as an imperfectly formed palate.

Without an opening from his palate into his nasal area, Dominic could not suck. A special bottle was formulated so their little guy could be fed. When his strength grew, surgeons stitched a seam across the top of his upper mouth. Since sucking develops the muscles for speech, Dominic started speech therapy at eleven months before he had even said his first words. The timing was perfect, and his first words formed correctly, resulting in no future speech defects.

Meanwhile, Tom and Julie decided to move to a new neighborhood to get a fresh start and leave behind the difficult memories as well as neighbors who introduced Julie as the mom who lost three babies.

One day as Julie was boxing up linens for the move, she walked past the guest room with a stack of folded towels in her arms. Taylor's nursery had been redecorated as their guest room, but the bedroom still featured several dolls propped up against the pillows of the double bed.

A little girl with brown hair was playing with one of the dolls. The girl turned toward the doorway and looked toward Julie. "I'm okay, Mom!" she said.

The image vanished as quickly as it had appeared in her mind, but an incredible joy flowed through Julie's heart. What a gift as well as a reminder that her daughter would be waiting for her in heaven, a fact she knew was confirmed by this vision. That day, Julie was freed from their home. She was not running away from the past but was choosing not to carry their losses into every day of their future.

A New Addition

It was nine years after her first pregnancy, when Dominic was five years old, that Julie determined she could go off of the birth control pill. Three years later, she became pregnant. She was well into her first trimester when Julie realized the fatigue she was feeling might be caused by something other than balancing work and motherhood.

This time around, though, there were no complications. Vince was born without a problem.

Both boys were told about their sisters in heaven. The girls' birthdays were remembered each year with a small celebration, and the first ornaments on the Christmas tree were always for their sisters.

Years later, Julie was carpooling to school when Vince said to his friend, "I miss my baby sister."

"I didn't know you had a sister. What happened?" his friend asked.

"Oh, she was born before I was, so I didn't get to meet her," Vince said. "But I still miss her anyway."

Julie accepts the fact that there will be no prom dresses or mother-of-the-bride experiences for her. After reading the book, *Heaven Is for Real* by Todd Burpo and Lynn Vincent, she felt the need to apologize to her third baby for many things.

In her prayer time, Julie confessed to her child that she was in a bad place when she lost her. "We didn't name you or even announce your departure," she acknowledged. Privately, Julie has given this little one a name.

"Taylor was born for us to hold every so briefly," Tom said. "The others are safely in God's hands. He's named them perfectly."

Julie can feel how God has been with her every step of the way. "I love the picture of God holding me in the palm of His hand," she said. "Can you imagine how big that hand is? You had a plan, Lord. I just couldn't see it."

Thoughts to Ponder

- Consider reading *Heaven Is for Real.* If you did not name your baby, consider the name God might have provided.

- Start a prayer journal. Talk to God in your journal about any guilt, anger, or frustration that arrived on your doorstep when grieving the loss of a baby before birth.

- Ask God to bring alongside you a listening friend, possibly another mother who has experienced a miscarriage. Let her take your hand and help you rise out of the depression or darkness you are experiencing.

About the Mother: Julie Bendinelli

Julie recently celebrated her twenty-fifth wedding anniversary with Tom. While Vince is just is in elementary school, Dominic is attending Point Loma Nazarene University in their hometown of San Diego.

Julie currently leads a Bible study, while Tom continues in sales management for a medical device company. Together they enjoy sports and hiking with their boys as well as special times as a couple traveling to various locations.

SECTION TWO

THE STRENGTH TO CARRY ON

5

"Don't Forget Me!"

Siblings' Response to their Sister's Long Illness and Death

Girls and their horses!

There seems to be an innate longing within many young girls to climb onto the back of a powerful stallion, galloping through open pastures with hair flying behind them and gracefully jumping over barriers with tail-swishing and mane-flying, finishing the ride with exhilaration that horse and rider are one.

So it was with Georgia Newton. She and her younger sister, Wynnie, and stepsister Evelyn—nicknamed "Sale"—shared a love for horseback riding as well as participating in equestrian events. Georgia and Wynnie were the daughters of Charlene Short, who had been an elite New York model before marrying her fashion photographer husband, Phillip Newton. They moved from the Big Apple to Seattle, where they both found work rather easily. Not long after arriving on the West Coast, Charlene became pregnant with their first child, Jack. Three-and-a-half years later Georgia was born, followed two years later by Wynnie.

Unfortunately, their marriage didn't last. Philip and Charlene separated shortly after Wynnie's birth, and the couple divorced soon after. Both retained equal custody of the three children and made sure they lived in close proximity to each other so that they could each maintain father-and-mother relationships in their children's lives.

While Georgia was quiet and shy, Wynnie was the crazy clown

who could bring a smile to the grumpiest of faces. The sisters were close because they shared a bedroom growing up, but Georgia's tidy, organized side always stood out to the cluttered mess belonging to Wynnie.

When Charlene remarried after falling in love with Emery, they had a Brady Bunch family on their hands. Emery came into the marriage with three children of his own. The union of the two families brought hope of a fresh start.

Georgia and Sale were the same age, and when they were eleven years old, these responsibly minded girls convinced their parents that they were ready to have a horse of their own. One day, Emery drove both of them to a nearby horse ring to look over a particular steed that had been advertised as being appropriate for young riders with limited experience.

The horse was brought into a ring for Emery and the girls to look over. "Would anyone like to go for a ride?" the owner offered.

"Georgia, you go," Sale said, even though she was the more experienced rider.

"Can I?" Georgia could barely contain her excitement.

Georgia mounted and began to confidently trot around the ring. Within seconds, however, everything went wrong. Without warning, the horse bolted and galloped feverishly around the ring. Georgia lost her balance as her foot came away from the stirrup. She tumbled forward, hanging on tight to the reins, but the quick forward motion caused her helmet to slip backward, exposing her forehead. Then the horse bolted again, causing her loose helmet to come off. Before anyone could calm the runaway steed, Georgia was thrown from the horse. Instead of landing in soft dirt, her head struck a tree root with a thud.

In an instant, Georgia lay prostrate on the ground, not moving at all.

An Emergency Situation

The phone rang at the house. Charlene was with Wynnie and fourteen-year-old Jack, who was battling a throat infection. The date was July 15.

When Charlene heard Sale's screams on the other end of the line, she didn't need a mother's intuition to know that something terrible had happened.

In the background, she heard her husband telling Sale, "Just tell her to come now!"

Charlene raced to the nearby farm and arrived as paramedics were stabilizing her daughter for transport to a nearby hospital. The ER docs quickly determined that Georgia needed a higher level of care. Georgia was airlifted to Seattle's Harbor View Hospital, the only Level One Trauma Center in the five western states.

For three weeks, Georgia remained unconscious in the PICU (Pediatric Intensive Care Unit) at Harbor View. Her family maintained a bedside vigil the entire time, taking turns reading to Georgia, playing music, and talking about her brother and sisters and what was going on at home. When her doctors suggested moving her to Seattle Children's Hospital for better care, the family received more bad news: their catastrophic insurance did not cover that kind of long-term medical treatment. Washington State had a Medicaid program for children who were hospitalized for a minimum of thirty consecutive days, but Georgia's stay of just over three weeks did not qualify her for state assistance. Thus, the family's request for Medicaid was denied.

Georgia's condition had shown little improvement. The parents believed that Harbor View administrators had informed Seattle Children's that she had little chance of recovery. As the thirty-day threshold for Medicaid neared, Harbor View recommended that Georgia be discharged from the hospital and be placed in the rehabilitation unit of a pediatric nursing home. Charlene refused, believing her daughter's best chance of recovery lay in receiving medical care, not rehabilitation.

In the midst of these agonizing days, a ray of light entered their lives through an angelic pediatric nurse intern by the name of Vicki, who steadfastly encouraged Charlene and Phillip to keep Georgia at Harbor View long enough so that she could qualify for Washington's Medicaid program. Vicki promised to do everything she could on her part to keep Georgia at Harbor View.

As the hospital was preparing to dismiss Georgia, the badly injured preteen caught a break of sorts when she developed a MRSA infection where the tracheotomy tube entered her neck. This challenging setback required she remain at the hospital for treatment. Thus, access to the state Medicaid program became available as the infection mandated she stay in the hospital's care through the weekend. Almost magically, the following Monday she was transported to Seattle Children's. Georgia now had the financial coverage that would give her access to the specialized teams at Children's Hospital.

Family members, friends, and coaches from Georgia's various sports teams all participated in a visitation rotation so that Georgia was never left alone. Three months after her tragic fall, however, and one-and-a-half more months at Seattle Children's, Georgia remained unconscious.

With the all-consuming task of running back and forth to the hospital, Charlene came to the conclusion that Georgia would best be cared for in their home. She asked to be trained so that she could facilitate Georgia's care in more familiar surroundings. In early October, Georgia left the hospital, attached to all the life-sustaining equipment necessary for her comfort. Seattle Children's Home Care Division provided the medical devices as well valuable answers to the family's concerns.

The first big decision Charlene made was to convert the family dining room into a makeshift hospital care unit. Nurses came during the day for the first month, but Charlene hated having the caregivers in her home. Jack and Wynnie were uncomfortable as well and sometimes hid upstairs most of the day.

"The nurses really didn't do that much, and I never trusted any of them to be with Georgia alone," remarked Charlene. "My stepmom, Dad, and my former husband, Phillip, would rotate staying overnight to help me out. It was a personal choice we made as a family. We decided we would take care of Georgia ourselves, even though there was a lot that needed to be done with her IV feeding tubes and changing her antibiotic lines every two to four hours. We just never slept. Also, I wanted to make things as 'normal' as possible for Jack and Wynnie."

Keeping Things Going

As part of Children's Hospital health care program, Jack and

Wynnie were offered free counseling sessions with a "child life" therapist experienced with catastrophic accidents. Neither sibling chose to meet with the counselor.

"I was starting high school that fall and trying to block out what was going on with Georgia," Jack said. "When Georgia was at Harbor View, I never visited her. I did go to visit her at Children's but ran off. The hospital was a tragedy factory, and I couldn't make myself go inside. I knew the whole thing sucked."

Wynnie, a few years younger than Georgia, was initially unsure how serious the horse-riding accident was. "The day of the accident was a blur," she said. "I was nine, and for the most part, I was kept out of what was happening."

Wynnie wasn't allowed to visit Georgia while she was hospitalized, which left her with a deep sense of loss. "Georgia was my best friend," she said. "My sister was always on the shy side, and I on the other hand was loud and extroverted. We balanced each other out perfectly, which is why it hurt so much when she was in her coma and couldn't communicate with any of us. I was cut off from my other half."

During the Thanksgiving holiday, Georgia surprised everyone when she moved her left arm up and down. Charlene was even more astounded when she thumb-wrestled with Georgia on the first day she moved her arm. Progress continued even though she had severe ataxia—uncoordinated movements—and couldn't sit up on her own.

Within weeks, though, Georgia rallied to the point where she partially regained use of her left arm. She taught herself to write with the left even though she was right-handed. Charlene was amazed when Georgia spelled out a description of the bald-headed ambulance attendant who cared for her on the way to Harbor View. She gave the titles of every book Charlene had read to her and recounted who had been at her bedside.

Georgia continued to communicate about her awareness while in a coma at the hospital. She knew what others were doing and saying. Recalling a particular nurse at Harbor View who had recited a hopeless prognosis to the family, she remembered Charlene taking the nurse aside and admonishing her not to verbally relate negative reports in front of Georgia, even if she did appear to be in a deep sleep. Innately, Charlene had known that her daughter was aware but unable to communicate.

Staying Apart

Georgia had always been a quiet, independent self-starter. The frustration of her limited expression and movement was the worst of all worlds for this young girl. Her unique personality was now unreachable. Although the frontal lobe was pristine, the trauma to the cerebellum and brainstem was extensive.

Much of the time, Georgia was out of control. The doctors described her as missing a "sensitivity chip."

After the accident, Wynnie separated herself from their mutual friends. She chose to attend a new school where no one knew the Georgia-Wynnie duo. Since their mutual friends were dealing with the loss of their best friend, it was easier to stay apart.

Distraction was Wynnie's ally. Despite her parents' hesitation, she continued her horsemanship and spent much of her time at the barns. Riding was an escape from a difficult life at home where Georgia's presence couldn't be ignored. Being in the saddle allowed her to feel normal.

Wynnie formed a close attachment with another rider named Elena. Although she had trained with both Wynnie and Georgia, Elena had not known them well but now played an important role in Wynnie's adjustment to Georgia's condition. Elena became the "amazing" friend who helped her focus on new beginnings.

"I don't think I ever really dealt with my situation," Wynnie said, "and I realize that I chose to distract myself and pretend that everything was normal. I think it was a good thing I kept my life going. Georgia's accident had brought so many drastic changes. The only option was to fall apart or keep moving on with my life. I never rebelled or acted out because I numbed myself by distancing myself from Georgia."

Wynnie still stubbornly resisted regular meetings with a therapist, even after she acquiesced and agreed to see one for a couple of sessions. "I thought the best thing for any child going through a situation like mine was to keep life going and focus on a hobby that was independent and separate from the situation you find yourself in," she said.

Georgia's presence in the family became more pronounced. Her moods would swing dramatically from serene beauty to depression and to anger and cursing. For instance, when Charlene would approach her gently in the morning and ask, "Georgia, do you hear me?", the response would often be a middle-finger gesture. When Georgia used a large-scale keyboard to communicate, she often typed out demanding statements such as "I want food!"

Charlene, as her mom, was consumed with "fixing" Georgia. She threw everything she had into Georgia's care and could fit nothing else into her life—and that included Wynnie and Jack. She never considered the impact on their lives as Georgia reigned in the dining room for months on end, which caused Wynnie to separate herself. Jack sensed that he better keep busy with soccer and high school classes. Life with a volatile Georgia became the new normal in their home.

A little more than a year after the accident, Georgia became very lethargic. When propped up in her wheelchair, she would do her daily exercises, but even this light physical therapy routine tired her quickly. On Halloween, a group of Georgia's old friends unexpectedly dropped in. They told Georgia about all the exciting things going on in their lives—including all the little romances at school . . . typical girl stuff. When they left, Georgia proceeded to destroy everything she could put her hands on.

"What's the point?" she typed on her computer.

The loss of hope weakened Georgia. Her declining strength became more and more apparent. In the second week of December, in response to a medical episode, Georgia was rushed to the emergency room at Children's Hospital. Doctors performed tests and determined that she had developed a fungal abscess in her brainstem, inoperable because of the location of the mass.

This young girl who had always loved to eat started refusing her meals. Her breathing was impacted, and it was apparent that Georgia was wasting away. It seemed Georgia knew she would never be independent and that her quality of life would be very low. The Ethical Care nurse wrote down the twelve-and-a-half-year-old's wishes: "Do not resuscitate. No more surgeries."

At that point, a massive infection was spreading. Georgia felt safe in the hospital listening to her music. Care dogs were brought in. Jack, in a turnaround, would come from soccer every day to receive his "I love Jack" cards from Georgia. This was a first.

For two weeks either a nurse or Charlene slept next to Georgia in her bed. Then one morning she wrote on her keyboard this short sentence: "Want to go home!"

Wynnie was appalled. The idea of Georgia dying inside their home was too scary to imagine, but her sister's wishes were respected. When an ambulance drove up to their address and paramedics wheeled her back into the dining room, Georgia was ready to go. She typed an emotional last request to her mother— "Don't forget me!"

The next day she was sleeping peacefully. Charlene called hospice. Georgia wanted the equipment turned off. She gave a thumbs up to "Jacky Boy." She asked Wynnie to come to her, and she said her goodbyes. Everyone was at the house. Phillip and Charlene stayed by her side until she peacefully passed away.

A Longing Perspective

"Georgia should not have lived," Jack says today. "What was she saved for? The one-in-a-million chance that she could get better? The whole family was impacted. Her brain injuries caused psychosis, OCD, violent behavior. She could not go to the bathroom by herself, nor sit up. She suffered continuously."

More thoughtfully, Jack added, "Selfishly, I am grateful for the time I had, but for her it was agony. Everyone has his or her own "bad." Georgia's accident gave me a deeper appreciation of living life well. It put little irritations in perspective. I find other kids' intolerances so trivial. I'm still dealing with a lot of loss. In a short period of time, so much disappeared from my life. It's hard to grasp."

Wynnie feels that the day of Georgia's accident was not just the day she lost her sister, but also the day she lost a part of herself. "Our relationship after the accident, through the hospital stay and during her rehabilitation, was never the same because Georgia was never the same," she said. "The sister I knew and loved was gone. In my perspective, although sad and hard to admit, the day of the accident was really the day Georgia died."

Wynnie has noticed that since Georgia's accident, her relationships with her peers and friends have changed. "I keep my true emotions and feelings to myself. I don't think this means I'm damaged or a worse person because of it. The main takeaway for me is that the type of change that comes from the loss of a sibling, especially a close one, is inevitable but not necessarily bad.

"I would like to tell children and teens going through a situation like Georgia's accident to try not to focus on acting normal, even though I realize that nothing will be normal after the loss of a sibling. Change happens. The process of grieving can be confusing, lonely, and hard to navigate. I lost Georgia twice, so I never expected anyone else to understand, which separated me from others. I do not recommend isolating oneself as I did, but it did shape who I am today. I am more aware of others now. I realize things are never as easy as they might seem and how impossibly unfair life can appear. But I have faith in the fact that although it is hard and confusing, your life goes on and you will be okay."

Charlene's Choice

While tending to Georgia at Children's Hospital on a daily basis, Charlene observed the aftermath of other families as they dealt with the loss of a child.

"I made a commitment not to lose the whole ship," she said. "One unit of their lives was unraveling, but I knew I needed the energy to pour back into my surviving kids. Hospice provided excellent grief support, but I witnessed how surviving children were basically kicked to the curb. I saw mothers lost in their own pity, unable to see the needs of their other children, who sometimes fell into drugs or ran away from their problems. I watched and determined that my family would not walk in the shadow of death. That determination gave me the motivation to pick myself up and continue on for my kids. It's a choice, and I made it."

Charlene admits that she felt guilty when she stopped dreaming about Georgia. She said she felt like her daughter was moving further away and she couldn't navigate the distance between them. The holidays were always the hardest because she wanted to buy presents for the *three* children, not two.

"This is reality," she concluded, "but the most important reality I faced was that Georgia was gone and I had two children who were growing up very quickly and needed to have their mom back. Georgia will not be forgotten. How could she think she would be forgotten? I honestly feel that the most loving way we can honor Georgia is by not squandering our time on this earth. We understand how precious time is, and we don't take our relationships for granted. We choose to remember the Georgia before the accident when she was her true self. Accidents are just that, not meant to be. I will never forget the strength she possessed when all else was out of her control but I can determine to remember the Georgia who loved riding in the ring, releasing her and me from the memory of the fall."

In the Seattle Children's Hospital Chapel, there's an eight-inch thick book that has recorded the name of every child who was cared for and ultimately passed away. On the day of Georgia's death, on the last page of this particular thick book, were the names of ten other children who had perished as well.

Life and death are a mystery in the hands of our almighty God. Charlene, Wynnie, and Jack celebrate Georgia's life and are determined to live their lives to the fullest.

Thoughts to Ponder

- Encourage your children to use a journal to capture the memories of their sibling that has died. Recall how his or her life impacted and changed yours for the better.

- Determine as a family how not to forget their brother or sister when he or she was alive and well. You can use articles of clothing to make a stuffed animal. Collect photos for a memory book with each family member writing his or her perspective on the photos.

- Consider a group counselor at your church or hospice who will encourage conversation around the guilt and anger that can be suppressed during a crisis in the family.

About the Family

Wynnie is a high school junior who volunteers with an equestrian rehabilitation program known as Little Bit, where Georgia rode for a short period. Wynnie says she feels comfortable assisting and encouraging the disabled children enrolled in the program. While considering where to attend college, she is preparing for her SAT and ACT tests and the college admission process. Jack is twenty-three years old, majoring in business at a college in Washington, considering marketing and advertising for his future career.

Charlene developed a children's skin care line called Budhi Baby, which she sold before signing on with a creative advertising agency called KIDs. After Georgia's death, the family dedicated a bench in Volunteer Park, where the Newton children spent lots of playful times when they were small.

Georgia's name is on the bench plaque, Charlene said. "There's not a day that goes by that I don't think of her, and I know she is always in our hearts," she said.

6

A "Dear Friends" Letter Rekindles Friendships

Do's and Don't's for Friends Eases the Isolation of a Death after Losing Son to Cancer

They met on Bruin Walk, the central plaza of the UCLA campus in Westwood.

"I hear you want some tennis lessons," Richard Eisendrath said to the petite eighteen-year-old UCLA freshman standing alone in the quad. Richard was feeling the pressure of work and pre-med studies at UCLA when a friend told him that his sister might type his term paper in exchange for a tennis lesson. When he wasn't grinding his way through organic chemistry and general biology classes, he was earning tuition money teaching tennis at the Sand and Sea Club, a beach resort in Malibu built for Charlie Chaplin's mistress, Marion Davis. Thus the pitch from Richard, a tournament-level player, to this cute coed, Diane.

"I'm pretty busy right now and generally I don't instruct beginners," he said, "but . . . if you could type my term paper that's due tomorrow, I could give you a one-hour lesson. That's only if you want to."

Did she fall for it? Of course. Athletic herself but not a tennis player, meeting her brother's friend Richard was an opportunity to learn the game from an exceptional coach and an attractive young man. He delivered the term paper that night at midnight; she had it all typed out for him the following morning.

Richard's side of the bargain didn't go as smoothly, at least in Diane's eyes. During their lesson, she was frustrated by his unwillingness to hit the ball directly to her. Instead, he made her run from one side of the court to the other and seemed to be amused by how uncoordinated she was on the tennis court.

Richard was just trying to have a little fun, but Diane would have nothing of it. She marched off the court. Richard, apologizing at the rate of a thousand words a minute, gave chase, but Diane held her head high and returned to her college dorm room.

The first encounters of a lifelong relationship are often humorous. The circumstances of a couple's first date and the ensuing cat-and-mouse courtship are the heartwarming stories passed along to the ensuing generations. It didn't take long for Diane and Richard to move beyond tennis and term papers to a solid partnership, knitted together with an indivisible bond that would be tested to its limits nearly three decades later.

Diane was raised in a strict Catholic family. When she decided to drop out of UCLA and move in with Richard—who also quit college and his dreams of becoming a doctor—both sets of parents were shocked. But the young couple was anxious to get on with life. When Diane's father realized their relationship was a serious commitment, he arranged for the both of them to work in his successful plumbing business.

Diane became a project manager of large government projects for the United States Navy Reserve airbase in Long Beach, California. In addition to the plumbing business, Diane's family also rehabilitated residential properties.

Richard learned everything about plumbing and the construction trade from the ground up and was put in charge of a small housing tract. After successfully selling the houses, Richard and Diane decided this was a business they could run together. Nearly six years into their relationship, they decided to get married . . . and her mother would finally set foot in their home.

Richard and Diane Eisendrath's first major purchase was a beachside residence in Oceanside, California, originally built in 1927. The shower and bathroom were outside the main house, but the sandy beach was a half block away. Every morning this young couple would check out the surf, assessing the best waves for boogie boarding. They entered Pro-Rider's competitions and often won their divisions.

They purchased their Oceanside home for a song and would net hundreds of thousands of dollars when they sold this beach-area residence years later and moved inland to Vista following the birth of their first child, John.

Their new comfortable home was the fulfillment of Diane's dream of living in a yellow rancher with a white picket fence. The property was in foreclosure, offered at an exceptional price, with enough acreage for a tennis court. The game that originally brought Richard and Diane together regained its focus at the center of their recreation. They joined the local tennis club where close friendships were formed, and they expanded their family. Three years after John was born, Becky arrived, followed three years later by Michael. When John was eleven, Mathew joined the family.

John was your typical first-born, doted on by his parents. He was one of those kids who would catch on to a joke immediately and laugh right along with the adults. He didn't enjoy school, and did just enough schoolwork to get by. When he started his junior year in high school, a classmate named Nicole, a good friend since elementary school days, made a bet with him: "Twenty bucks says you can't get straight A's this semester."

She was on. After John aced his classes and brought home a clean straight-A report card, Nicole had to pay up. When Diane heard John bragging to a friend that he had easily won twenty dollars off Nicole, she made him give the money back. He paid her $15, saying he'd done the work and should get some reward!

For his senior project, John wrote a paper on how to be a successful real estate agent. After all, he'd grown up seeing his parents buying and selling homes, speculating on the real estate market and refurbishing properties for a profit. Soon after graduation, he studied for his real estate license and passed the state test. He became one of the youngest real estate agents in San Diego County. He gave all his former teachers gift cards from Starbucks with a note saying, "Think of me when you want to sell your house!" Working side by side with his father and mother brought a closeness that was very meaningful.

By twenty-two, John was living life in the fast lane. At one point he owned a BMW *and* a Mercedes. His bank account totaled more than $200,000. With eighteen listings and several high-end deals in the works, he was well on his way to becoming a very rich young man. Then the scourge of easy money and rapid success ripped his life apart after a friend introduced him to OxyContin, a painkilling prescription drug. He quickly developed an addiction.

His body demanded the drug and soon required greater quantities to satisfy his desire. In less than a year, he blew through his $200,000 in savings on a drug-fueled escapade. When the money was gone, John would cross over the border into Mexico, frequenting dark alleys to hock a computer or a cell phone to meet his needs. Back on the U.S. side, he was involved in five car accidents, totaling his car as well as the rental car provided by his insurance company.

His driver's license revoked, his resources completely depleted, John's only choice was to move back in with his family. Being highly regarded in their community, Richard and Diane struggled alone, keeping their personal issues to themselves. They determined, though, that they must intercede for John's life.

Into Rehab

The call from the local jail was the final humiliation for Richard and Diane. Drug addicts attract drug-addicted friends, and so it was for John. He and his crazed girlfriend had previously filed for restraining orders against each other after their relationship ended. The allegations included mutual physical abuse. After leaving rehab, his obsession with this relationship led him back to her apartment in a quest for solace and more drugs. An argument ensued, however, and she called the police. John was arrested and taken to a holding cell. Calling his mom and asking her to bail him out of jail brought the realization he had hit rock bottom.

On John's twenty-fifth birthday, Diane arranged for a group of his old friends—people she knew weren't into the drug lifestyle—to celebrate the occasion. When the party was over and everyone had gone home, she sat face to face with John.

"You need to go to McDonald Center and get yourself off of this drug," she declared. "It's destroying you. You are smart enough to know it! If you choose not to go, your family has decided to do an intervention and take you there. Please John, make the right choice today, your birthday." Diane begged her son to find the strength she knew was within him.

He agreed and the Monday after his birthday, he checked himself into the McDonald Center, a residential drug rehabilitation program developed through Sharp Hospital.

As everyone expected, the first five days of detox were excruciating. John called Diane, begging his mother to "Get me the @#$% out of here!" Many of the counselors were former addicts themselves who personally knew the body's compelling urge to be appeased.

Following the McDonald Center program, John checked into the Sober Living facility in Del Mar. His parents arranged the best room possible, and together they worked to keep John drug-free. In his rehab classes, John met heads of corporations, physicians, and anesthesiologists who were in the midst of treatment for their own issues with drugs. That's when John realized that addiction impacted the most competent of individuals. He listened well, progressing through a twelve-step program that emphasized a power source outside himself. John chose Jesus Christ as his power source.

Meanwhile, Diane attended Al-Anon meetings to cope with her feelings of guilt and responsibility. She had questions: What could she have done to prevent her son's addiction? Had the way they parented John provoked a need for drugs? Had they been too lenient, given him too many things growing up?

Diane prayed daily for her son to find the strength to stay

with the program and be released from his chemical dependency. She was told, however, that relapse often happens after rehab. She hated hearing that, but that's how it went for John as well. Within a few weeks of moving home, John was using again. Diane was encouraged, though, when a woman and her son from the Sober Living center convinced John to return to the program. After three months, John's life was transforming. To stay busy and earn some money, he continued to do paperwork for his parent's company. He talked about saving enough money for a down payment on a house.

At twenty-seven, after two tumultuous years battling addiction, John returned to work full time. An amazing transformation was taking place. John sought out new sober friends. His mom brought him back into tennis, arranging doubles games at the club where John filled in as the fourth. He and his dad played weekly with a group of Richard's friends. Diane encouraged John to assist her in instructing some of the younger children of her tennis buddies.

Much like his parents, John loved sports and became engaged with teaching others. He also took up golf and really enjoyed playing 18 holes with his new friend, Dick, an eighty-five-year-old gentleman who loved John like a son.

When he wasn't on the courts or at the driving range, John kept busy with the family real estate business, seeking out new listings and showing homes to potential buyers. John counted each day as a victory, constantly aware of how easy it would be to slip back into his old lifestyle—and how painful the recovery would be. Staying clean would be his journey for the rest of his life.

He and the family had been told that less than 5 percent of drug users successfully got clean. John was one of those fortunate

5 percent. He did everything he was counseled to do in the Sober Living program, regaining his driver's license, getting his misdemeanor for battery waived, and his record clean.

It wasn't easy. He never drove a car in the six months he was without a license. He made all of his court dates, paid all his attorney and bail bond fees, and reimbursed his mom and dad for every penny he had borrowed from them. His sense of achievement was matched only by the pride his parents took in their son's new life.

Freedom Ahead

John's desire to stay clean and his fear of being prescribed medication kept him from seeking medical attention for aggravating bowel and stomach pains that plagued him quite frequently. He told his friends that dealing with "a few bouts of persistent discomfort" was better than struggling with prescription meds.

For the first time in years, Diane was experiencing more freedom in her life. John and Michael were living on their own, Becky had completed her senior year in college and was job hunting, and Matthew was driving himself to and from Cathedral High School, a private Catholic high school a forty-five minute drive away.

For years, carpooling kids all over San Diego had been Diane's life, but with Matthew able to fend for himself, Diane had time to become more engaged in the family business. She also talked with Richard about John taking on more responsibilities, which would allow them time to travel together.

Early one morning, while Diane was sipping coffee and

daydreaming about a future trip, the phone rang. John was hurting.

"Hey, Mom, my stomach is in knots," he said. "I'm really in a lot of pain, but I don't want to see a doc!"

Diane was aware of John's concern about medications. "Let me come pick you up," she offered. "I'll go with you to the clinic. Seeing a doctor doesn't always necessitate pain medications."

The doctor recommended a series of tests, one of which showed a very high blood count in the liver. Their insurance company gave clearance for a CT scan, and they were off to urgent care. The next few hours waiting for the results seemed endless. Richard came from the office to join them in their vigil.

"Of course, it's a hernia or an ulcer," Diane said. She had always been the family member with the positive attitude. When they were told the doctor would see them, Diane told John and Richard to go ahead. She preferred to sit in the waiting room and pray. When Richard came out of the office twenty minutes later, however, his face was so gravely sad that Diane thought he was faking and would do his usual turn about and give her a big smile. *This face must be a joke, like he always does to me*, she thought hopefully to herself.

There was nothing to smile about. The doctor had detected a tumor and scheduled a biopsy for the next morning. John was told to fast for twenty-four hours.

The following morning, a biopsy report showed that cancer originating in the colon had metastasized to the liver. The news came as a bombshell and shocked all three of them. Driving home in silence, Diane asked John, "How about some Chinese food tonight?" This was their favorite take-out food to share together.

"Sure, Mom," John replied. "Sounds really good."

They were all trying to be brave that day. When their meal was finished, no one wanted to take a fortune cookie. The outlook for the future was stunningly dim.

After that trip to the doctor, John never went back to the home he had purchased just three months prior. The bedroom he occupied as a child became his home once again. Becky was a tremendous help to Diane, driving John to his treatments and spending precious time with her brother, something she was available to do because she hadn't yet found a job following graduation from college.

Diane kept meticulous records of John's medications. When speaking with different doctors on call, she realized they did not always have the details of John's situation. Had she not kept a record of his daily ablutions and become his ardent advocate, John's care would have been haphazard. Due to his former addiction, pain maintenance required stronger and stronger dosages. His body had become inured to the impact of meds. Moreover, his appetite was sporadic. A cheeseburger would sound appealing but, with a smile, he would caution his mom that he might change his mind when she returned with a plate containing a burger off the grill and pan-fried potatoes.

Having a twenty-seven-year-old at home all day became a challenge. Diane decided they would focus on creating, making things grow. She bought numerous plants, and together they planted a garden surrounding a freshwater Koi pond in the side yard, just outside John's bedroom. His strength faltered, but each day he had a reason to wake up to complete their mutual project.

Then John learned that he was terminal. There was no hope

that he'd beat the cancer, but John wasn't going to give up. He submitted his cancer-ravaged body to chemotherapy, which further weakened him. He and his mother also sought help at UCLA and USC medical centers as well as Moore's Cancer Center.

Every day Diane went to Mass at Saint Francis Catholic Church in Vista. She would ask every person she met to pray for her son's healing from cancer, including the rather large gentlemen who claimed the left corner of the front pew with a large, dog-eared, leather-bound Bible in his lap.

"Sir, would you pray for my son John to be cured of his cancer?" she asked one day.

"Write his name here in my Bible," he kindly replied.

Diane wrote John's full name on the front flap of the Bible, joining numerous other prayer requests. "Thank you," she responded.

"Bless you," he said.

John hated the fact that his family home, typically filled with laughter, was lifeless like a tomb. Friends visited less frequently. One day, though, a friend stopped by and innocently regaled John about the annual Halloween party at the club, which the Eisendraths had never missed. Diane saw John looking at her accusingly, as if to say, *You should have been there with your friends.* John saw his family losing their joy.

One day John's friend's Chad stopped by to visit. John was in the process of completing the sale of his home. He said to Chad, "I think when I sell my house I will buy a sports car. I will know I have made it when I own a sports car; a 911 Porsche would be just the car for me."

The next afternoon, when Chad drove by John's house he saw

a brand new black 911 Porsche in the driveway. Chad smiled as he thought of their conversation the day before. John had "made it!" Later John took Chad for a spin and told him when he drove his Porsche he felt no pain!

Despite the happiness of that moment, John started slipping away. He was sleeping most of the day, numbed by the medication masking his pain. He had no appetite for food. Diane gently asked him, "All your girlfriends are calling. Is there anyone you would like to see?"

John asked for Robyn, who happened to be a hospice nurse and was one of the only friends Diane trusted to leave John alone with. After visiting with John, Robyn quietly encouraged the family to bring in hospice to assist the family.

Diane resisted the idea, but Richard felt it was time. Much to Diane's surprise and delight, hospice sent a Carmelite nun named Nadine to attend to John . . . and Diane.

When Diane shared with Nadine the details of her son's illness, the nun's eyes were moist with tears. "I've been praying for a young man named John for quite some time," she quietly shared. "An older man named Michael, who sits in the front pew at Saint Francis, showed me a name written in his Bible. He asked me to pray for a young man named John for healing from cancer. I have been praying for your family. Now I have the opportunity to be here with you at the end," Nadine said.

Only God could have orchestrated such a coincidence that could bring amazing comfort to Diane as well as the knowledge that God had provided her with a praying friend.

That afternoon another young woman replaced Nadine, but the following morning Nadine returned. She joined Diane in John's room.

"Good morning, John," Nadine said cheerfully.

There was no response. Diane was aware that even though the body is shutting down, a person can still hear. In fact, hearing is one of the last senses that those on their deathbed lose. Diane continually talked to John about mutual friends and the times they had together as family members gathered around.

Nadine checked for a pulse, then exchanged a knowing glance with Diane. His pulse was almost undetectable. Diane gently laid next to her son for his last moments here on Earth. The entire family gathered around his bedside, but during his last ten minutes, Diane lay close and prayed for her son as he slipped peacefully from this earth to Heaven.

A Time to Plant

Planning the burial services kept Diane busy through the following week. She wanted the memorial to be perfect: a tribute to her brave son. But when the busyness ended, she was driven by the need to stay occupied. Diane, a typically high-energy person, started planting pots. Purchasing, planting, watering, and feeding—the frenzy she threw into this new project began to worry her family. When she had several hundred plants to tend, a neighbor kindly brought her a set of orange buckets to transplant groups of smaller pots into the larger containers.

When she didn't have her hands in dirt, Diane baked cookies, dozens at a time, and watched every religious DVD she could put her hands on. She wrote in her journal, organized John's medical notes into binders, and printed and catalogued all the Caring Bridge entries she had written as well as the many responses from friends. No activity could fill the void in her heart.

Diane attended bereavement groups and befriended another grieving mother who introduced her to Umbrella Ministries, a Christian support group that brings together mothers who've experienced the death of a child. There she met mothers further along on their grieving journey. She saw they were able to laugh again and spoke of the comfort they found from the Lord.

"I was attracted to mothers who had 'the light,' " she said. "The light is the joy that can finally come back into your life. It's really not complicated. I guess it's the doing that's hard, but I call the doing the trust, taking the first steps. First with hope, then faith, then the trust part, and finally the doing," she recalled. "There's no progress if you don't DO!"

Richard encouraged Diane to get back on the tennis court. Hitting the ball hard released pent-up frustration and provided some sense of relief. She had been volunteering instruction for children during John's illness and decided to resume the lessons.

She noticed, though, that when she and Richard went to the club, friends they had known for twenty years were uncomfortable encountering them. At a loss for the right words of comfort, they unwittingly hurt Diane and Richard more by avoiding them. At the grocery store, Diane would notice a friend turn her cart quickly into another aisle to avoid a sensitive conversation.

One night in the wee hours of sleeplessness, Diane decided she would provide good advice for her friends. Another mother shared with her a letter that had been written just for this purpose. Diane called it "The Don't Letter," and when she asked the owner of their tennis club if she could post it on the activities board at the front entrance, he readily agreed. And the letter was posted.

A "DEAR FRIENDS" LETTER

Dear Friends,

Unless you've lost a child, then DON'T ask us if we are over it yet. We'll never be over it. A part of us died with our child.

DON'T tell us they are in a better place. They are not here with us, where they belong.

DON'T say at least they are not suffering. We haven't come to terms with why they suffered at all.

DON'T tell us at least we have other children. Which of your children would you have sacrificed?

DON'T ask us if we feel better. Bereavement isn't a condition that clears up.

DON'T force your beliefs on us. Not all of us have the same faith.

DON'T tell us at least we had our child for so many years. What year would you choose for your child to die?

DON'T tell us God never gives us more than we can bear. Right now we don't feel we can handle anything else.

DON'T avoid us. We don't have a contagious disease, just unbearable pain.

DON'T tell us you know how we feel, unless you have lost a child. No other loss can compare to losing a child. It's not the natural order of things.

DON'T t take our anger personally. We don't know who we are angry at or why. We lash out at those closest to us.

DON'T whisper behind us when we enter a room. We are in pain, but not deaf.

DON'T stop calling us after the initial loss. Our grief does not stop there, and we need to know others are thinking of us.

DON'T be offended when we don't return calls right away. We take each moment as it comes, and some days are worse than others.

DON'T tell us to get on with our lives. We each grieve differently and in our own time frame. Grief cannot be governed by any clock or calendar.

~ ~ ~

DO say you are sorry. We're sorry, too, and you saying that you share our sorrow is far better than saying any of those tired clichés you don't really mean anyway. Just say you're sorry.

DO put your arms around us and hold us. We need your strength to get us through each day.

DO say you remember our child, if you do. Memories are all we have left, and we cherish them.

DO let us talk about our child. Our child lived and still lives on in our hearts, forever.

DO mention our child's name. It will not make us sad or hurt our feelings.

DO let us cry. Crying is an important part of the grief process. Cry with us if you want to.

DO remember us on special dates. Our child's birth date, death date, and holidays are a very lonely and difficult time for us.

DO send us cards on those dates saying you remember our child because we do.

DO show our family that you care. Sometimes we forget to do that in our own pain.

DO be thankful for children. Nothing hurts us worse than seeing other people in pain.

It's been said that a wife who loses a husband is called a widow. A husband who loses a wife is called a widower. A child who loses his parents is called an orphan.

But there is no word for a parent, a stepparent or a grandparent who loses a child.

That's how awful the loss is.

The Eisendraths' friends appreciated the posted letter. The phone rang once again and friends reached out to embrace the family in their loss. Since then, the "Dear Friends" letter has been widely circulated among grieving families. While the journey of grief is unique to every person who loses a child, their need for understanding and acceptance is the same.

Thoughts to Ponder

- Is there someone you need to forgive for ignoring you in your grief? Write a letter of understanding to your friend, acknowledging the discomfort they experience and sharing your insight into what has helped you on your journey.

- What activities could you "do" as you grieve the death of your child? Could you find an area of your yard where you might plant a memory garden?

- Is there a sport you have neglected after your loss? Call a friend to walk with you, play tennis, or take up a new activity to revive your energy.

About the Mother: Diane Eisendrath

Diane continues to work in the family business. All her children are continuing in the footsteps of their parents in the real estate field.

Six months after John's death, Diane uncovered the black Porsche and went for a ride. They were going to sell the car to a gentleman who responded to their ad, but they decided to keep the sports car in the family.

Umbrella Ministries has brought Diane into contact with several mothers whom she ministers to in their grief. One of those moms' boyfriends turned out to be the person who almost bought John's Porsche.

Diane attends Bible Study Fellowship every week, learning how God sent the Holy Spirit to be the one, true Comforter for our losses here on earth. The uplifting prayers of her Bible Study leaders miraculously brought Diane out of the fog of depression. She now brings God's light into the lives of other moms who have experienced the death of one of their children.

7

Working Through Forgiveness

A Letter to a Murderer Sets Her on a Path Toward Healing

If you had asked Mickey Pease what her passion was when she was a twenty-five-year-old teacher, she would have replied that her goal was to encourage and guide young minds—including her children. She and her husband, Jack, who was preparing to enter a Ph.D. program for his doctorate in child psychology, looked forward to starting a family of their own.

While praying for their family to begin, her husband came upon a Bible verse—Isaiah 60:4—promising "their sons would come from afar and their daughter shall be nursed at thy side." Mickey and Jack began to prepare for the children they were confident God would provide—whether naturally or through adoption.

A local doctor contacted Mickey and Jack regarding a young patient who was looking for a couple to adopt her unborn child. Claiming Isaiah's promise, the nursery was decorated in shades of blue anticipating the arrival of their son-to-be. Andrew Pease was their first adopted child.

Andy, as he was affectionately called, was a precious gift. Born with two club feet, he adapted to the casts on his legs, which quickly molded his little feet into those of a runner. He was a chatterbox who found a friend on every playground and encouraged stray animals to be his pet. His menagerie included snakes and rabbits, hamsters and dogs. As a little tyke, he loved to swim and play soccer and baseball. When he grew bigger and stronger, he acquired a love of football, at which he was quite talented. As the first child, Andy had Mickey's undivided attention, and both parents devoted themselves to their adopted son.

When Andy was four, Mickey became pregnant and delivered a baby sister, Sarah. Their young family was blossoming. Then the opportunity arose to adopt baby David and, two years later, baby Jonathan. God had been true to fulfilling His promise.

"School, here I come," was Andy's chant as he marched into kindergarten. Discovering books brought a new excitement to his young life. At first, his favorite books were about animals. As his interests broadened, the encyclopedia became his bedtime reading choice. His first grade teacher reported his reluctance to go out for recess if a marvelous new book captivated him. Although struggling with a spatial learning disability that impacted his math skills, reading kept him motivated in school.

Several job relocations ultimately brought the Pease family to Vista, California, where Mickey returned to teaching and completed her M.A. degree in Instructional Leadership. After Andy entered Vista High School, his prowess on the football field attracted a broad group of friends as well as a sense of self-confidence. Friday nights under the lights brought the entire family together in the stands cheering for their adored big brother. But off the field, Andy was keenly aware of a struggle within his parent's marriage, which made him unsure about his future.

A Family Rift

For several years, Andy's mom had been holding the family

together financially. His father was fired from a construction job for mishandling the purchasing of supplies. While Mickey struggled with bouts of depression, Jack chose to arbitrarily retire from all employment, which set the family down a dangerous path. Andy perceived the rift growing between his parents and chose to enlist in the military when his parents separated and ultimately ended their twenty-two-year marriage. For Andy, the U.S. Army would provide the structure and security his home was now missing.

Physically fit from his years of playing football, Andy thrived in the military. While stationed in Honolulu, he enjoyed time with his buddies at the Army canteen where they relaxed and danced. One particular evening, he caught the eye of a lovely young woman, Christian, who proceeded to cut in on his dancing partner. She thought he looked like Phil Anselmo, the front man for Pantera, a rock band that Christian loved.

From that moment on, Christian did not want to let him go. She had found a tall, blond, handsome man in uniform. It wasn't long before the two found themselves deeply in love. She told friends that she was instantly comfortable with Andy, as if she didn't have to "add water" to their budding relationship. They were soul mates who'd known each other for years.

The stress of the Army marching and training routine magnified the weakness of Andy's ankles, a fragile area due to the corrective measures required for his club feet. After sustaining two broken ankles, Andy was medically discharged after just three years of service. With the military behind them, Christian and Andy decided to marry and begin their family in Northern California.

Healing and Reunion

At thirty-three, Andrew, as he now chose to be called, was progressing toward a degree in history from Humboldt State University while working part time as program director for troubled teens at the Boys and Girls Club of the Redwoods in Eureka. His family with Christian now included two sons, Caleb and Ethan, who adored their fun-loving dad and the outdoor life they shared together. They enjoyed the beach, camping, and playing Frisbee golf. In the mornings when Christian and Andrew were having their coffee in front of the TV, the boys would waken and run downstairs, then pile on the sofa for a time of wrestling and tickling before they all snuggled in together. Christian was Andrew's soul mate, and their life together was sealed in love.

With little warning, however, Andrew was diagnosed with thyroid cancer. Treatment ensued and after a two-year battle, he was declared cancer-free. With a renewed sense of gratitude for life, he decided to seek Mickey's help in finding his biological mother. Working through an Internet reunion site, Andrew entered his name, the year of his birth, and the town he had lived in. One of the names listed matched a young woman on a website for their local high school. Andrew sent an email asking the woman if she had given birth to a boy on June 4, 1972, in their city. Would she respond if she actually wanted to meet her son? The birthmother responded positively, and the reunion was a joyous occasion for the entire family.

For Andrew, life was good in his mid-thirties. With his cancer in remission and being only two units short of a history degree that would facilitate his goal of becoming a teacher, he was enjoying family and friends. He was motivated to provide for his family no matter what the job. He made pizza, washed dishes, took the bus, or walked to work to be sure his family's needs were met.

Christian had a positive influence on Andrew, encouraging him to finish his college degree. When he got a job with Jazz Kids, a residential home for autistic children, he felt fulfilled in his desire to make a difference in young lives. With flowing locks, a youthful outlook, and loads of patience, Andrew was a natural fit with the developmentally delayed teens.

Andrew's love for Christian never dimmed during the peaks and valleys. One time, when Christian was down with the flu, Andrew stopped by a vacant field and picked a handful of wildflowers that he gathered into a bouquet, a symbol of how he was thinking of his soul mate for life.

Something Unexpected

On an evening in early February, Andrew helped serve dinner for the youngsters under his care at Jazz Kids. Since it was movie night, Andrew volunteered to go get snacks for the special entertainment. Together, he and one of his closest charges—a fifteen-year-old autistic boy—drove the short distance to Ray's Food Place, a local supermarket, to make their selections.

According to a Eureka Police Department criminal investigations supervisor, the department received a report of an attempted robbery near the 1900 block of J Street at about 5:40 p.m. The victim told the dispatcher that he had been riding his bicycle down J Street when two men tried to steal his belongings, then assaulted him.

That report was followed by a robbery outside a Jack in the Box fast food restaurant on Broadway, then another one in the parking lot behind the Bayshore Mall, all within thirty-five minutes of the original call. Witnesses at each robbery reported that one of the suspects was brandishing a knife, and the pair had fled in a white Volkswagen Jetta.

Shortly after responding to the call at the mall, officers were again dispatched, this time to investigate a report of an assault with a deadly weapon in the parking lot of Ray's Food Store, just a couple of blocks away. There they encountered a fifteen-year-old boy hiding behind a car. In the middle of the pavement, Andrew Pease was lying in a pool of blood, dead from more than a dozen stab wounds.

Family Notification

Around 10:00 p.m., the doorbell rang at Andrew's home.

Christian wondered who could be there at this late hour. Andrew was due home at any moment.

She opened the door and saw a uniformed officer from the Eureka Police Department standing on the landing. He asked if he could come in.

Christian felt unsteady as she took a seat on the living room couch—and then was horrified to learn that Andy had been murdered. Two young men were being booked in the county jail.

The first phone call she made was to Andrew's mother.

"What will I do without Andy?" Christian sobbed into the phone as she tried to tell Mickey that in an instant of insanity, her son was gone, her grandsons were fatherless, and she was now a widow.

Mickey Pease could not fathom the evil that had occurred that fateful February evening. No human understanding could rationalize or accept the brutality of her son's death—repeatedly stabbed over and over. A totally senseless crime.

Questions that had no answers plagued her: *Did Andy cry out? Was he desperately afraid? Did he feel the thirteen stabs of the knife into his body and ultimately into his heart?*

Over and over, her anguished mind replayed the scene. And she wondered: How does a mother who is herself brokenhearted begin to comfort her daughter-in-law and young grandsons?

Throughout her life, Mickey had memorized Scripture. The Psalms had sustained her through the devastation of her divorce, and once again she found herself holding onto God's words to bring her the fortitude she needed to console Christian and the boys.

Scanning the Psalms of David and the New Testament words of Christ, strength coursed through her body like blood running through her veins. Psalm 34 quieted Mickey's ravaged heart as she repeated the promise of the Lord's closeness and the lifeline that only His Spirit offers. She memorized those lines most uplifting to help sustain her in her moments of deepest despair.

These three verses were most often repeated by Mickey:

- "My soul clings to you; your right hand upholds me." (Psalm 63:8, NIV)

- "The Lord is close to the brokenhearted and saves those who are crushed in spirit." (Psalm 34:18, NIV)

- "For I know the plans I have for you," declares the Lord, "plans to prosper you and not to harm you, plans to give you hope and a future." (Jeremiah 29:11, NIV)

Andrew had been instantly taken up into the arms of the Lord in the land of the living: of this Mickey was certain. The painful reality was here in the land of the dead. How could healing come out of this darkness?

James Robert Stanko was sentenced to a prison term of twenty-six years to life for the first-degree murder of Andrew Pease. The District Attorney said that his office had entered into the plea agreement with Stanko at the behest of Christian Pease, noting that she did not want to deal with the pain of sitting through a trial. She wanted Stanko to admit his guilt. A tape recording was played of a jailhouse conversation that Stanko had with his mother in which he confessed to having killed Andrew Pease. Drugs and alcohol had propelled James Stanko's life into a downward spiral that hit bottom that fateful evening when he led the crime spree that ultimately took Andy's life. The tone of the tape recording was one of deep regret and remorse.

Christian Pease addressed the court and the convicted Stanko with an emotional statement challenging Stanko to consider the life he had taken—that of her husband—and robbing her of the chance to grow old with the man she loved and the children they were raising together. "Our two boys will never be able to grow up doing the simple things in life with their father," she said through a jumble of tears.

Dealing with Forgiveness

The imminent incarceration of James Stanko offered little peace to Mickey's aching heart. The morning before the court sentencing, she tried to focus on her morning devotionals. Reading but not retaining, she pushed herself to keep seeking the comfort she so desperately needed. The words of Jesus transcribed by Luke in Chapter 17:3 from a King James Bible literally leapt off the page. She read them a second time:

"Take heed to yourselves: If thy brother trespass against thee, rebuke him; and if he repent, forgive him."

Was she being asked to forgive the murderer of her dear son? Would the act of forgiveness bring a sense of release and peace to her tumultuous emotional state of the past three months of hearings? Mickey sat down with a blank sheet of paper, and the words flowed from her heart. What transpired was a letter from a mother to a murderer, which was read at the time of sentencing. Here is what was said in court:

Dear James Stanko,

Today I looked at my son's picture and burst into tears, sobbing because we can never again hear his voice, see him play with his children, love his wife, or pursue his dreams. I kept saying in disbelief that HE IS DEAD!

Your actions have changed our lives forever. His sons will never play games or have fun with my son. His wife must experience tears and pain every day as she attempts to provide for her young family, without the support and love my son gave her. We no longer are the same family; each of his siblings is missing him in different ways, and of course his dad and I have huge holes in our hearts.

Then there is the young autistic child, excitedly going with Andrew to get goodies for a movie night, hiding behind a car, watching and listening to you murder his buddy, friend, and surrogate father. He is ruined forever by your actions. And I think of the wonderful woman who tried to stop you with her car, watching in horror as you cruelly murdered my son.

My son is in another place where he is now whole, happy, and doesn't have to live in pain or try to combat the sin in this world. But you, you are a part of this world and must pay the consequences for your sin and heinous actions. For the next many years, you will live a captive life, not enjoying your family or friends, nor pursuing your goals. By murdering my son, you too have been murdered by your own actions. You will have decades to contemplate your choices in this life.

I firmly believe that this life is but a birthing process for eternity, and the choices we make determine where we spend eternity. God sent His Son, Jesus, for you and for me. We have all sinned and fallen short. God wants you to come to Him, accept the forgiveness Jesus has to offer and live the rest of your life in a relationship with Him.

I guarantee you that there is nothing more satisfying in this life—in prison or out. I pray that you will find this peace in your soul, for you must be experiencing much pain and anxiety for your behavior and how that night changed your life forever too.

I am praying for you.

Mickey Pease
Andrew's mother

Forgiveness Comes in Many Forms

It may be hard to imagine offering the means of salvation to the very man who murdered your child, but as Mickey would tell you, what is our choice? To be swallowed up by hatred brings our own destruction.

Mickey was not demonstrating that she was the better person. Her heart cried for her son and for his dear family. Nightmares of his murder plagued her. She asked God all the "whys"—like when Andrew's life was just beginning to turn around, when years of discouragement had transformed into hope for his future, and when he had overcome thyroid cancer, why did this random event have to happen?

But her soul recognized a lost man. Her son will spend eternity in heaven; this man will spend the rest of his natural life in jail. The hope for our future is, moment by moment, to turn our emotions over to our Creator so that He can miraculously comfort us and give us His vision for our lives. Receiving His love gives us the strength to reach out to others, including one whose wretched act robbed us of a loved one.

He who counts every hair on our head and understands our every need can cleanse bitterness, hatred, and darkness from our lives. The rock of support is His word. He will reveal the perfect plan for our life. Even those of us whose lives are etched with a large hole can be led out to find healing and renewed purpose.

"I just kept thinking that if Andrew died that others might come to know Christ, then all would not be lost," she said.

Building a Legacy

Andrew left a legacy for his family that will provide for them every month. Because he was on the job when the stabbing occurred, Christian is receiving worker's compensation that has allowed Christian to return to school, furthering her education in order to better support herself and the boys. Humboldt State University posthumously awarded Andrew's BA degree in History. Upon presentation, the entire audience of graduates and their families rose and gave Christian a standing ovation.

Every summer, Mickey arranges a return visit to Eureka to conduct "Camp Grandma," a special month of adventure with her two grandsons and her granddaughter. They snuggle in the evenings and share memories of their wonderful father that often result in tears. But that's all right. It's like they feel the comfort of resting in the warmth of Jesus' tender arms.

Andrew provided one last gift to his family. A few months before his death, Andrew left a voicemail message for his mother. His unmistakable voice said, "Hi, Mom. Just checkin' in. I'll be home. Give me a call."

That voicemail wasn't deleted before his death, and it won't be deleted in the future because each time Mickey listens, she's taken back to other conversations that she and Andrew shared over the years.

Mickey received God's forgiving grace as a young adult. Never did she imagine that in the receiving, her heart would be softened to the point where she could extend that same unmerited forgiveness to the murderer of her son.

For Mickey, the act of forgiveness was a gift. In the giving, she was freed from the bitter grip that hatred held on her heart and her life. In receiving, James Stanko knew he had been given a gift he did not earn or deserve.

Finally, she clung to this teaching from the Apostle Paul:

So we are not giving up. How could we! Even though on the outside things are falling apart on us, on the inside where God is making new life, not a day goes by without his unfolding grace. These hard times are small compared to the coming good times, the lavish celebration prepared for us. There's far more than meets the eye. The things we see now are here today gone tomorrow. But the things we can't see now will last forever.

—2 Corinthians 4:16-18 (The Message)

Thoughts to Ponder

- Consider opening your Bible to the Psalms and hearing God speak through David's relationship with God. Highlight or underline those that speak encouragement to your heart.

- Write a letter of forgiveness to someone whose sin has brought devastation to your life. Pray for God to change your heart toward this person.

- Think about the most precious treasure from your child's life on earth. It could be a drawing or a handwritten little note or thoughtful card. Consider sharing this with a close friend and relating the circumstances that make this a prized memory.

About the Mother: Mickey Pease

Mickey grew up with a contentious father, a strict disciplinarian who wasn't afraid to use strong physical punishment. The transformation of her heart through committing her life to Jesus prompted her first act of forgiveness—reconciling their father-daughter relationship just two years before his death.

She's now dedicated to educating young minds. After teaching first grade for one year, Mickey joined the staff of Campus Crusade for Christ (now known as Cru), working with students on campuses across the United States. Mickey earned a M.A. in Christian Ministry and returned to teaching with the Vista Unified School District while completing her M.A. degree in Instructional Leadership.

Retiring in 2004, she flew to Kashgar, China, to teach the children of British and American missionaries. Two years later, she traveled to Astana, Kazakhstan, where she fell in love with the hearts of the Kazakhstan people. Andrew's death occurred while Mickey was in the U.S. making arrangements to return to Kazakhstan for a longer duration.

Mickey's daughter-in-law, Christian, encouraged her to continue her mission to teach English in a country whose people she had grown to love. "Andy often spoke of your teaching with pride. He would not want you to give that up to stay with us," Christian told her. Currently, Mickey is in Kazakhstan teaching English to children and their teachers. Her life is a testimony to the love of God that continues to heal her and allow her to minister in her profession.

"God has been more than faithful as I have experienced His warm, comforting arms around my body and soul," she said, "urging me on toward the goal I believe He has set before me—living a life for the betterment of others."

8
It's God!
A Family Fights
Against the Power of Drugs

ADDICTED TO LOVE

Your lights are on, but you're not home
Your mind is not your own
Your heart sweats, your body shakes
Another kiss is what it takes
You can't sleep, you can't eat
There's no doubt, you're in deep
Your throat is tight, you can't breathe
Another kiss is all you need
Ohh oohh

These lyrics to Robert Palmer's song, "Addicted to Love," describe the seductive power of the body's craving for pleasure. Whether it's love, prescription drugs, or heroin, a powerful need for short-term gratification drives repetitive, compulsive behavior despite adverse consequences and deleterious effects.

Any mother who witnesses the transformation of a gregarious, loving child into an irritable, anxious, angry young man experiences extraordinary pain. Janet LaDue's story shares the challenge facing a family whose child is addicted. There's a fine line between tough love and enabling, and this mother's struggle to find that line drew her to God's lasting comfort.

Janet and Randy LaDue welcomed redheaded "little" Randy into the world just two years after their romantic wedding in Puerto Vallarta, Mexico.

Janet had met her future husband when she visited a girlfriend attending San Diego State University, where Randy was enrolled as a student. She was introduced to Randy at a party, but it wasn't until she moved to the San Diego area that they started dating and fell in love.

A seventeen-day trip was planned to explore Mexico, with the culmination being their wedding in the interior gardens of Puerto Vallarta's La Casa de Oro Hotel; the perfect spot for their lifetime commitment. With a justice of the peace presiding and a waitress as their witness, they determined their love was forever and stronger together, a knot that would not be unraveled. The birth of Randy was a fulfillment of their dreams for a family.

Their firstborn was all boy. His animated freckle face expressed all the energy contained within his pint-sized frame. He loved playing outdoors and creating his own adventures—either in the backyard or on the various camping outings with his folks. When Randy turned five, his brother Jonny arrived on the scene, completing the family circle.

Surfing, skateboarding, and fishing comprised many father-son outings. Hiking and camping excursions and lots of road trips to many different locations knit this family together with lifetime memories. The boys' father, Randy, loved these family adventures because of his upbringing in a dysfunctional home.

Raised by an alcoholic father and grandfather who both died from alcohol-related accidents—and a mother who was a recovering alcoholic—Randy was keenly aware of the possibility that he might have the same tendencies for substance abuse. As a young man, he had offered a prayer for insight asking God, "Lord, if I'm an alcoholic, please give me physical proof."

As the old saying goes, sometimes you need to be careful what you pray for.

For a time, prior to their son's birth, Randy and Janet enjoyed sharing a few beers with neighbors and friends. One evening when those "few" became a few too many, Randy blacked out and fell through the railing on their deck, severely scraping his back in the fall.

When Randy awoke the next morning, he felt an excruciating pain in his back. He took a look in the mirror to see what was hurting so badly and realized that he had been given the proof he had been praying for. Randy took a picture of the severe scrape on his back as a reminder of the dangers that alcoholism represented. This was his proof. The following day, Randy started his journey with Alcoholics Anonymous. The photo of his injury remains in his wallet today.

School Daze

When little Randy was in the second grade, he complained repeatedly about his teacher. He hated going to school. One morning, Randy's dad had had enough of the morning battles. With notebook in hand, he accompanied his son to school so that he could see for himself what was happening in the classroom. Right off, Randy noticed that the teacher, a well-intentioned man, was attempting to befriend each of his young students. He did so by tolerating behavior inappropriate for the classroom.

One visit was enough. Janet and Randy had been attending Horizon Christian Fellowship in suburban San Diego each Sunday and were aware that their church had a K-12 school on church property. Their concern was the cost of private school since Jonny would be following his older brother. That month, though, Janet had made their last payment on their BMW, which turned out to be a godsend. The cost for Horizon School was exactly the same as the car payment they had been shelling out monthly for several years. Christian schooling would definitely fit into their budget now!

The results were exponential. Randy loved Horizon School. Janet helped in the classroom and felt God's presence in the teaching. When Randy reached junior high, he joined the Missions Team, a group that offered him the opportunity to serve those in need via projects just over the border in Mexico.

Randy and his younger brother Jonny had distinctly different personalities. Randy was more effusive. He loved to talk. As a youngster, he held his mom's hand while they rode along in the car, relating a tale of riding a big wave or describing a touching experience that happened on a missions trip. Exuberant Randy was constantly wanting to do more. Jonny was the quiet one who looked up to his older brother and liked listening to his brother's latest adventure.

The Teen Years

Surfing was Randy's passion. When he turned sixteen and got his driver's license, he began working at a surf shop where he associated with an older group of kids who were surfers. Jonny, an impressionable eleven-year-old at the time, liked to hang out with Randy's buddies as well. One evening after the shop was closed, the sales rep for a wetsuit company passed around beers, including the minors. Randy joined in the beer drinking. Jonny was the tattletale. He told his parents what had happened, and in turn, they shared the information with the surf shop owner. The news didn't make the owner very happy nor did it make Jonny very popular with Randy's friends.

The impact of the surf culture—and its propensity for drinking and drugs—proved to be detrimental to Randy. Horizon High School had a no-tolerance policy regarding drugs, so when a baggy of marijuana fell from Randy's pants pocket, he was expelled immediately. Jonny was uncomfortable staying at Horizon since the hallways reverberated with whispers about Randy's expulsion.

In an attempt to gain more influence on their lives, Janet began home schooling both boys. Randy rebelled by cheating on the tests. He wasn't too smart about hoodwinking his mother, however. When he consistently scored 100 percent, it was obvious that he was stealing the answer sheets from his mother's desk. After a lock box failed to secure her materials, the decision was made that Randy had to enroll at their local public high school.

With the added independence, Randy began to spiral out of control his senior year. A series of skateboard and surfing injuries introduced him to the highly addictive painkillers Valium and Percocet. Extreme mood swings became a frequent occurrence. Randy managed to graduate from high school and enrolled at a junior college, all the while using prescription drugs and smoking marijuana.

The cycle was debilitating. When he wasn't at school, Randy worked at the surf shop shaping and repairing boards, after which he would smoke dope, go surfing, and party at night. When his parents confronted Randy regarding his poor choices, he would become defensive and angry, sometimes even violent, smashing the drywall of his bedroom with his fist and leaving gaping holes. When his parents told him that he had to move out, he promised to quit drugs and stay clean.

Janet had no idea the extent of her son's addiction. Even with the family history, she did not understand how addiction controlled Randy's behavior. Even though his heart was sold out for the Lord, his mind was controlled by drugs.

Everyone who knew Janet well had an opinion about what she should do.

"Tough love is the answer," one friend counseled.

"Just keep lovin' on him every day," offered another friend.

"He'll come around. It's just a phase kids go through," advised another.

One thing Janet did know. The erratic behavior could not continue in their home.

Taking Action

It was time for an intervention. The first step was getting Randy into an outpatient clinic, where he was required to see a counselor three times a week, participate in group therapy sessions, and be drug-tested weekly.

These therapy sessions brought unintended consequences, however: Randy was placed in elbow-to-elbow contact with kids much more sophisticated and street smart than him. They taught him how to beat drug tests and introduced him to new suppliers. After many failed attempts to stop using drugs through out-patient counseling, Randy was sent to an in-patient facility in Los Angeles for treatment. A week into treatment, Randy exhibited signs of an extreme anxiety attack and was allowed to go to a nearby emergency room, where he was given a highly addictive anti-depressant drug called Klonopin.

Klonopin was not allowed at the in-patient facility, so the next day, the facility director put him on a bus back to San Diego.

Upon his return to his old stomping grounds, Randy became very anxious again. He went to the very hospital sponsoring his rehab program and was given his anti-depressant drug of choice— Klonopin. No one checked further than his name on a former doctor's prescription. His addiction was back full force—and with a vengeance.

Janet could not allow Randy in the house. Forced to improvise, Randy began "couch surfing"—sleeping in the living room of anyone who welcomed him. One of Janet's well-intentioned friends felt so bad for Randy and did not understand how sick his addiction had made him. She wanted desperately to help him, so she did his laundry.

"How could you do that?" Janet asked her friend. "He has to hit bottom to finally realize drugs are his enemy."

One evening, Randy appeared at their home looking like a homeless bum. "Just a shower, Mom?" he begged.

Janet's in-laws were staying at the house. She, her husband, and Jonny were preparing to leave the next morning for a vacation in

Costa Rica. She felt such deep anguish for her son that she softened her conviction and allowed him to come inside for a shower. The in-laws agreed he could stay while the family left the country for a week. Within two days, though, the in-laws had to deny him access to the house. It was apparent that Randy was using again.

The following week, Randy returned to the house to retrieve his surfboard. His father refused to let him in because he was obviously under the influence. Randy shoved his dad aside, grabbed his board from his bedroom, and started swinging it in a threatening manner at his father, who fled the house. Randy chased after his father and backed him into a canyon behind their home.

In the midst of the mayhem, Janet called 911. She was terrified of what she saw in her son. The police arrived with their canine patrol while a helicopter circled over their home. The police counseled Janet that incarceration would give him seven to ten days to detox that would help him think straight, but in order to arrest Randy, they needed evidence of unlawful drug use. The dogs couldn't find any drugs, however, but when his dad searched his truck, he found another person's prescription for OxyContin, an addictive painkiller. Randy was arrested, which netted him a ten-day jail sentence—and a chance to detox.

Into a Deep Hole

Randy's dad was inconsolable that his son's life had spiraled out of control. He awoke in the middle of the night after dreaming that Randy had died. Weeping with despair, he cried out to Janet, "No one can help me. No one understands the pain of losing my son to drugs."

Janet reminded him of a wonderful pastor at their church named Mickey Stonier. "Go to Mickey," she said softly. "He'll understand. He'll pray with you."

Even though it was two in the morning, Randy was desperate to get help—or answers—about his son. He awoke Mickey in the middle of the night and then drove to his house, where the two talked and prayed until a sense of calm entered Randy's heart.

Later that morning, he visited Randy in jail. Sitting in a small visiting room, separated by a glass barrier, his dad asked, "Son, what's wrong?"

Randy looked back with vacant eyes and spelled out the word "heroin" on the glass.

Ten days after being in jail, Randy was released. He called home and spoke with his mom. His dad picked him up at a street corner. Since Randy was not allowed in their home, father and son spent the night in a local hotel. Together they discussed his options.

Randy had recently connected online with his fifth grade girlfriend, Betsy. He was honest with her and described what he had recently gone through. Betsy, a compassionate soul, was intrigued by his story. They decided to have lunch, where she encouraged Randy to check himself into Freedom Ranch, a ninety-day, county-run rehab program that could help him learn how to stay clean and sober and could help him renew his relationship with God. Located sixty miles east of San Diego in Campo, Freedom Ranch provided a social-model program where residents ate, studied, and worked with peers further down the road to recovery from drug and alcohol addiction.

Sober after his stint in the local jail, Randy listened earnestly to Betsy's encouragement to commit to Freedom Ranch's three-month rehabilitation program. Randy determined he had someone to live for and ~~he~~ wanted to get clean.

A Fresh Start

With prayerful support, the family drove Randy to Freedom Ranch. During the first thirty days, Betsy and Janet would visit the ranch and play cards with Randy. Betsy's letters were filled with Scriptures that nudged Randy back into God's arms. There were no cell phones at the ranch, so the letters and visits were a highlight. Entering the second month, Randy was feeling in charge of himself. As an adult, he could check himself out of the program, which he did. Provided with a bus pass, Randy headed home.

Parents experience a great deal of guilt when trying to muster the strength to stick with tough ground rules for a child dealing with addiction. This time when Randy appeared at the door, his father and mother welcomed their prodigal son to the family.

Come in! We love you dearly was the natural response of parents wanting to believe this time the sober life was a reality. Randy settled into his room and called Betsy to say hello. Minutes later, Randy called out, "Hey, Mom, I'm hungry. Should I run out and get some sandwiches?"

"Great idea," Janet said, who gave him some cash. "Go get yourself something to eat."

Instead of driving himself to the sandwich shop, Randy detoured to a nearby emergency room, where he complained of severe anxiety and asked for a "refill" of Klonopin, the exceptionally strong anti-anxiety depressant. The prescription was on file and filled. Randy used the cash his mother had given him for lunch to pay for the Klonopin.

Later than evening, he and Betsy got together with some old friends from high school to talk and have a few beers. The impact of just a "few beers" on a heroin addict had a multiple effect. When he came home on a drug- and alcohol-fueled bender, his parents were crushed with disbelief. A terrible argument ensued.

When things finally calmed down, everyone agreed that they should stop arguing and get some sleep. They could talk about things more rationally in the morning. Randy was allowed to stay another night, and then he was told to find somewhere else to go. He reluctantly left the next day. Betsy left the same afternoon for an out-of-town commitment. She called the house the following morning.

"Have you heard from Randy?" she asked.

When Janet replied no, they both knew something was wrong. In the past, no matter how bad the argument or how doped up Randy was, he called his mom and Betsy every day.

Janet told her husband about the disturbing phone call, and the two of them brainstormed about where he could have gone. His dad knew that Randy often went down to San Diego Bay where he'd crash with a friend on his boat. He and Janet drove to the marina where they saw Randy's truck.

They approached the vehicle and saw that all the windows were down. They could see his friend's boat from outside the gate. Randy's bicycle was parked on the boat deck, and his AA books and Bible were in the basket of the bike. They knew he was there, but the access gate was locked and the harbor attendant couldn't be found.

Frustrated—and greatly worried—Randy and Janet drove to a San Diego Police substation to file a missing person's report, mentioning the location of the truck and bike at the marina. Within an hour, the Harbor Police gained access to the boat, where they made a grim discovery—the dead body of Randy LaDue.

When the police called to deliver the heart-breaking news, Randy's dad answered the phone. Janet saw the shocked and pain-filled look on her husband's face. She screamed. She knew Randy was no longer alive. They were asked to come to the marina and identify their son. A friend was called, and he drove them to the marina. When Randy stepped out of the car at the parking lot, tears were streaming down his face. A policeman approached Randy, saying, "Sir, we've sent for someone to come and comfort you."

"No one can comfort me," Randy replied. "My son is dead!"

At that moment Randy looked across the parking lot to see the only person in this world who could offer solace in this moment. It was Horizon pastor Mickey Stonier's first assignment as police chaplain, having taken the job just a week earlier.

"Only God could bring to me the pastor who knows our family's struggle and now our loss!" Randy exclaimed. "It's truly God!" Then he buried himself in Mickey's comforting hug.

Toxicology reports would later indicate that Randy died of an overdose of heroin.

Comfort in Their Loss

Randy's memorial service was a testimony in itself. The deadly power of drugs and addiction was a gruesome reality for all the young people in the audience, yet the resurrection power of Randy's ultimate faith in the God of his salvation was proclaimed. Randy was free forever from the forces that drew him to his death.

Released from the battles of this life, he was heaven bound, free at last.

The impact of losing his older brother brought about severe depression for their son Jonny, who decided life was over for him too. Drugs would become his solace to the deep pain of loss.

Wiser and with more conviction than ever, Janet and Randy responded quickly to their fifteen-year-old's depression. Everyday for two weeks, the principal at The Rock Academy High School would greet him at the front entry and encourage him to persevere and find comfort with teachers and friends who loved him.

Jonny continued to struggle with depression and drugs for five years, going through trials that were similar to his older brother. He was in and out of different treatment centers. Jonny became involved with heavy drinking and smoking marijuana, as well as taking various other illicit drugs. This led him to helping a friend deal the drugs as well.

In a last tragic turn of events, Jonny's friend was shot and killed by the police, which turned out to be a turning point for Jonny's life. He finally hit bottom and reached out for help.

He was sent to Sober Camp at Palomar Mountain for two months: afterward, he resided in a sober living facility for another five months. Now, almost one year clean, Jonny understands the reality in his life. He has the gene of self-destruction; he cannot touch drugs or alcohol. Their power is stronger than his will but not stronger than his faith.

Janet and Randy erected a memorial bench on the cliffs above their son's favorite surf spot. One day when Janet found time to visit the site, she mused, "Is this all I have left of Randy? A bench?"

At that moment, though, she determined she was going to learn to enjoy this place. She set a routine where she would bring her praise music and devotionals, breathing in the beauty of the ocean before her. Janet had committed to leading a Grief Share group at her church.

Sitting on the bench one morning, Janet was recognized by a woman from her Grief Share group. They began talking, and Janet told her that she liked to sit on a bench dedicated to her son's memory.

"Oh, I hadn't made the connection," said the other mother. You know, this is where I go to read and pray about the loss of my brother. This is where I feel God's presence the very most!"

Praise God, thought Janet. *That's exactly what I want this bench to be.*

Thoughts to Ponder

- Seek a Grief Share group at your local church. Keep a journal of the positive steps taken by parents who lost a child from a drug overdose.

- Find a location at your home or elsewhere that was a favorite of your child's. Create a memorial that reflects the best times in your child's life.

- Visit an Alcoholic Anonymous meeting to be educated about the systemic power of drugs over the body. Acknowledge that as a mother you did everything in your power to prevent the death of your child.

About the Mother: Janet LaDue

Janet LaDue continues to lead Grief Share groups within her church. Randy's struggle and ultimate death allows her to share her experience of God's forgiveness and cleansing that leads to healing from the judgment and guilt experienced by families who lose a loved one due to drugs. Janet is actively involved with Umbrella Ministries and provides comfort to mothers whose loss is similar to hers.

Randy volunteers his time to recovery groups and has helped dozens of young people struggling with drug addiction. Both parents have dedicated themselves to using their loss to free other young people from the destructive power of addiction.

SECTION THREE

TURNING LOSS INTO LEGACY

9

She Chose to Heal

*Soothing Teas Created after the Premature Birth
of Twin Daughters*

Rachel stood in front of the bathroom mirror, shocked by the drawn, red-eyed image staring back at her.

Today would be the funeral for her identical twin daughters, Aubrey and Ellie, whose short lives had captured her heart and challenged her faith in the weeks they struggled for life. Her eyes filling with endless tears, she spoke to God. "Lord! You and I are no longer friends. I will do what You say, but I no longer believe serving You pays off!"

* * *

Having grown up in a Christian home as the oldest of three daughters, Rachel Crawford felt God's call on her life from an early age, confident that He would use her for His purposes. You could say that Rachel was "sold out" for the Lord.

As a teenager, she volunteered for mission trips to underdeveloped countries. Her dad preferred that she not tell him about the risks she encountered while reaching out to the poorest of the poor in isolated areas of the world. Her confidence in who God was and what Jesus did for mankind allowed her to freely share the Gospel with all who would listen. Her faith was grounded in the belief that God was a loving healer who sent His Son for all, especially for those who suffered and experienced loss. Of that, she was sure. She trusted. She saw lives lifted out of misery bringing salvation out of desperation.

Attractive, popular, and well liked, Rachel had little time for boyfriends growing up. The longest high school relationship she can remember lasted six weeks. Dating was not a priority. Her stomach would growl loudly and churn with discomfort at the awkwardness of a first date. All too often, there wasn't a second.

Her outlook changed in college when she met Kirk Crawford, who shared her passion for Jesus and was interesting to boot. Most importantly, her stomach was silent when they were together, a sure indication to Rachel that this was a bond made in heaven.

Rachel and Kirk married and were soon blessed with a pregnancy. When she went into labor, Rachel preferred to deliver without drugs, employing the services of a "doula"—a birthing assistant—who supported Rachel throughout her natural labor and delivery since Kirk, a military officer deployed in Iraq, couldn't be there. He finally saw their first child Dustin when he was three weeks old. Round rolls of baby fat soon appeared as Rachel nursed her growing son. For this young couple, all was well with the world.

Early in Rachel's second pregnancy, she and Kirk learned that a double blessing awaited them, especially because twins weren't found in the family lineage on either side. The pregnancy progressed normally until twenty-four weeks, when Rachel spent a day with annoying back pain.

The next morning, however, Rachel recognized that she was in labor with the twins. Kirk rushed her to the hospital. Because Rachel's labor had progressed so far, there was no time to give her steroid drugs to help with the development of the babies' lungs.

All attempts to stop her labor were unsuccessful. One tiny foot pushed to the outside of Rachel's body. Fearing infection, her doctors hesitated to push the small appendage back into the womb. Although the babies weren't due to be born until October 7, Aubrey was the first to enter the world on June 24, 2008—three-and-a-half months premature. Her sister Ellie was close behind. Each tiny girl weighed less than two pounds.

All illusions Rachel had of being in control slipped away. Having always believed she was living a life surrendered to God's will, Rachel felt a crack in her faith that day. She called out to God to help her babies. Serving God had been her insurance policy that all would go well in her life. Shouldn't that have been the payoff for living for Him?

Praying for a Pair of Miracles

The next hours and days were a nightmare. For three days Rachel hardly slept. She was running on adrenaline. The tiny babies were on ventilators, receiving blood transfusions, suffering brain hemorrhages, and showing signs of organ failure. They could not hold fluids, and it seemed that their frames were visibly shriveling.

Their doctors gently discussed with Kirk and Rachel what expectations they realistically might have for their girls. All the while, they prayed for miracles from God their Healer and for guidance from the Creator of all life. Because the impacted areas of the girls' brains controlled their eventual ability to walk and talk, Rachel had nightmares in which their souls were trapped inside bodies that could not communicate verbally or physically. She and Kirk weighed the consequences of the doctors' efforts to sustain the babies' breathing and weak heartbeats.

Ellie was the one to force their hand. When her small intestine erupted, surgery was considered but the doctor bluntly told them he doubted Ellie could survive such an invasive operation. On the evening of July 1, after just seven days of life, Ellie was removed from the machines, tubes, and tape. She was wrapped in a warmed blanket and held in her mother's arms.

In a quiet room, Mom and Dad captured the last moments with their beautiful Ellie. After a short while, abruptly, Kirk looked toward Rachel. She felt it too—like the air had been sucked out of the room. That was the moment when they both knew Ellie's soul had left her body.

Her heart had taken its final beat. Now she was in the arms of Jesus.

They walked together down the long hallway, surrendering the lifeless body to the waiting nursing staff. Plaster casts were made of her tiny hands and feet. Then Rachel and Kirk went to tell Aubrey her sister was gone. They were exhausted and left the hospital for home, hoping to gain strength for the days ahead.

Aubrey was a fighter, but that same night, she too experienced intestinal failure. Rachel and Kirk received a call at 1:30 a.m. asking for permission to transfer Aubrey to San Diego's Children's Hospital. The parents gave their approval.

The transport was hard on Aubrey. When she arrived at Children's Hospital, doctors determined she was too unstable to treat. Then a second brain hemorrhage occurred, impacting her brain stem—the area of the brain that controls blinking, swallowing, and breathing.

It took four more days for Kirk and Rachel to summon the courage to take Aubrey off of life support. On July 7, cloistered in a private room together, Rachel placed a swaddled Aubrey against her bent knees, looking down at her perfect face. Aubrey opened her eyes and wiggled inside her blanket, which broke Rachel's heart into even more pieces. After two hours and forty-five minutes, Rachel said to her wide-eyed little girl, "It's okay, Aubrey. You can go now." Within twenty minutes, Aubrey joined her sister in heaven.

Rachel was overwhelmed with grief. In the days that followed, her only answer to the pain was to call everyone on her phone list. Family, friends, and acquaintances were shocked to hear her voice conveying the terrible news of the loss. If there was no answer, she left a complete voicemail.

She was hungry but she didn't eat. Instead, Rachel kept making calls, compelled to be the one who told everyone the girls had died. She seemed to experience a sense of time warp: if she stayed on the phone, she wouldn't have time to feel. Although blessed with a wonderful family, Rachel realized that her self-sustaining, responsible life had left her without a real support group. The depth of her grief absorbed her completely.

On the morning of the funeral, Rachel stood in front of the bathroom mirror and told God how it was going to be between them in the future. Then she put on her dress and looked a second time in the mirror and declared, "This will not destroy my life. This will not determine who I am from here on out. *I choose healing!*"

Turning on her heels, she went to retrieve Dustin and join Kirk for the service they had planned in honor of Aubrey and Ellie.

Throughout the two weeks of the girls' short lives, Rachel had been pumping and storing her breast milk. As the weeks followed, she continued to store the vast supply that was coming from her body. After pumping and storing for seven weeks, the Crawfords' freezer was at capacity.

Gingerly, Kirk approached his still-grieving wife and said, "Rachel, we have to do something with this milk. It can't stay here forever."

Knowing that institutions were required to boil the milk to insure protection for the babies who would ingest it, Rachel did not want to lose the full value of the colostrum and life-giving probiotics contained in her breast milk. She could not bear to dump the highly nutritious breast milk down the sink.

She called her doula and asked if she knew of any mother in need of breast milk. At first the answer was negative, but within a few hours Rachel received a call back. A woman named Finola Hughes, already the mother of two adopted boys, had recently added a third child to her family. This time it was a girl named Sadie, who was six months old.

Although a beautiful baby girl, she was sickly. She was underweight and constantly on antibiotics, which in turn caused digestive problems. Sadie was labeled with a condition called "failure to thrive."

Finola was convinced that what her baby needed was breast milk. Through a series of coincidences—God working in disguise—she made contact with Rachel's doula. Within a day, Rachel was driving the breast milk, packaged with ice in multiple coolers, to Carpinteria, a coastal city 200 miles north of San Diego. Little Sadie took to the milk immediately. Within a month she was hitting her milestones, off all medications, and gaining weight and color in her chubby cheeks. Color also came back into Rachel's gray world as she experienced a positive, tangible blessing and a glimpse of God's presence once again.

She felt like God had taken her by the hand and joined her in her walk of grief by offering hope and a purpose in her life.

A Healing Cup of Tea

For Rachel, choosing healing was a daily decision that began with sitting on the couch and drinking a hot tea. Rachel loved tea. As she sifted through the heaviness of her healing journey, she found that her quiet times with a cup of tea brought solace to the start of her day.

Rachel's sister, Crystal, often dropped by to check on her and would find Rachel sipping a tea. On one such occasion, Crystal said to Rachel, "I wish there was something we could put in your tea to make you feel better."

"Now that's an incredible idea!" exclaimed Rachel.

Crystal's innocent comment brought an earnest look into her sister's eyes. After thinking a moment, Rachel said, "Crystal, I think we should create a line of teas for the various stages of grieving, with natural ingredients that add to one's sense of well-being. This would be something tangible we could give to a mother that would truly be a remedy for her heart and mind. Let's do it!"

One year later, after extensive research and experimentation with blends, Crystal and Rachel had their tea branded and ready for distribution. "Teamotions," a line of six tea blends, entered the marketplace. The image on the tea tins was a teacup cradled in a mother's arms. Hundreds of hours of investigation brought together blends of Indian Ayurvedic herbs, naturopathic remedies, and adaptogens all extensively examined for their health attributes. All the ingredients combined together with tea for a positive response.

In seeking out the soothing ingredients in Teamotions tea, the purchaser acknowledges her need for help. The process of healing is not as fast as others expect. The sipper of the tea is entitled to not be okay. Drinking tea includes the ritual of taking a moment in time to sit, to be still, to read, to meditate, or to write in a journal. The tea offers an elixir for hope, joy, strength, clarity, rest, and peace. The tea is a physical representation of the decision to heal. It is a symbol—an anchor to the need she recognizes at that moment. When she shares a cup of tea with a friend, she is no longer alone on the journey.

After the death of the twins, Rachel realized that her choice to heal required more than mental determination. As she allowed herself to consider how God could use her in this loss, she determined that He had something big in mind—a worldwide BIG! It was her hope not only to feel some sense of normalcy for herself and her family, but also to know that God wanted to use Aubrey and Ellie's short lives to be the impetus to change others.

Rachel knew that God could transform other people's hearts and health through her offering of comfort and hope. This tea was a means to an end, much like the power of Jesus' life to offer resurrection to a broken life here on earth. She recognized that everything, loss and gain, comes under the power of the resurrection. The devastation of this life is not the conclusion. The fruition of this life is yet to come.

Rachel knew that God wanted to use her knowledge of tea along with her experience of losing her precious daughters to bring health and healing through the solace of His love—and a simple cup of tea.

Thoughts to Ponder

- What talent has God given you that He is encouraging you to share with others? Are you an artist, a vocalist, an athlete, a writer, a cook, a baker, or a flower arranger? Each of us is blessed with unique gifts. Encourage another with the inspiration of your talent.

- Choosing healing is a decision. What have you decided for your life going forward? What one thing can you choose today that will make your life brighter tomorrow?

- Search the Book of Psalms for David's praises to the Lord. What specific thing in your life causes you to praise the God of our life? Make a list of praiseworthy life experiences.

About the Mother: Rachel Crawford

In July 2010, Rachel gave birth to her second son, Colton James, who reminded his mother not to live in fear. He is a chubby, cuddly, blond, blue-eyed tornado. Six-year-old Dustin, a kind, sweet, and smart little boy, is starting the primary school years. Rachel is confident God has special plans for both of her sons. She counts her blessings that real healing has taken place in her life.

Rachel and her sister Crystal continue the hard work of growing the Teamotions business. Rachel's husband Kirk, an officer in the Marine Corps, was promoted to major and was reassigned to Camp Lejeune in Jacksonville, North Carolina, where they will live for the next two years. She looks forward to planting a garden with her boys, getting their first Slip'N Slide, and positioning Teamotions to grow nationwide.

After the loss of Aubrey and Ellie, Rachel stopped dreaming big, but today her dreams have returned to her. That is a miracle in itself.

10

Signs and Songs from the Heart

Coincidences Empower a Mother to Make a Difference after Her Son's Suicide

"BJ" Jensen stood before her choir in silence, her twinkling eyes scanning the bright faces before her. The singers stopped fidgeting and paid attention; they knew their performance would begin in several moments—the instant BJ raised her hands and then launched them into the opening soaring melody. The choir's royal blue and periwinkle attire silently spoke of the deep faith and the beauty of the songs that BJ had chosen for this event.

Seated in the auditorium was a community of men and women who had experienced the death of a child. This was the closing ceremony, the climax to the week's program for grieving parents attending the national conference of the Compassionate Friends organization in Washington, D.C.

There would be no mention of Jesus or heaven. The group's secular stance precluded any religious presentations. Still, seeking God's infinite wisdom, BJ chose two pieces for the finale that reflected her conviction that these families needed to depart with the hope of heaven in their hearts. Waiting for the signal to begin, a smile spread across BJ's face as she personally dedicated the performance to the precious memory of her youngest son Jay.

Jay's Childhood

Jay Morgan—his last name came from BJ's first marriage—was born six weeks before his due date, the first of many surprising moments in his life. Following thirty-six hours of difficult labor that finally pushed his tiny body into this world, Jay was born with underdeveloped lungs—Idiopathic Repertory Syndrome—the same condition that took the life of Patrick Kennedy, the youngest child of President John Kennedy and his wife, Jacqueline, back in 1963. Patrick Kennedy, also born six weeks before his due date, died two days after his birth.

Fortunately for Jay, advances in neonatal medicine saved his life. Swept away from his mother before she could take him into her arms, Jay was hooked up to pumps and wires and had to fight for every breath while his mother watched and prayed him through two frightening weeks.

After his condition stabilized, Jay's two-year-old brother, Jeff, was ready and waiting for the arrival of his baby brother. They grew up to be best of friends. The two towheads shared a bedroom, toys, and adventures while developing their opposite natures. Older brother Jeff was reserved and cautious, while Jay was the spontaneous, outgoing, and fun-loving one. Jay's lack of organization drove his "neatnik" brother to draw a line down the center of their bedroom so that Jeff's side could have order—hung-up clothes, toys in their place, and a made bed. Jay's mind, full of fantastic adventures, had no time for cleaning up. His half of the room resembled the aftermath of a tornado.

At times Jay was a wonder to his family. At an early age, Jay could add, subtract, divide and multiply double figures in his mind.

When Jay was just five years old, Jeff asked his mom, "How long will it take me to buy a GI Joe if I save all my allowance every week?" No sooner was the question out of his mouth than Jay blurted, "Five-and-a-half weeks!" Then he exclaimed, "Wow! I just saw that in my head!"

As he entered grade school, Jay was captivated by baseball, memorizing the statistics, batting percentages, and jersey numbers of the players on his favorite team—the Chicago White Sox. When BJ arranged a trip to Comiskey Park in Chicago, Jay tucked his most treasured Carlos May trading card in his just-the-right-size shirt pocket. As he patted his prized possession to be sure it was secure, the biggest, most grateful smile spread across his face—a moment engraved in his mom's memory forever.

Arriving early to the park, they discovered that Carlos May was signing autographs outside the White Sox dugout. The excited little devotee was full of anticipation as Jay and his mother worked their way to the railing.

"Sorry," said an usher as he stepped in front of them. "No more autographs today. No exceptions." They watched Carlos May jog out to his left field position to shag a few balls.

Dejectedly, they turned, hand-in-hand, to walk back to their seats. Jay broke the silence as he innocently inquired, "Mom, what's an autograph?"

Smiling, she explained that an autograph is when someone writes his or her name on a piece of paper, such as his baseball card.

Quiet for a few seconds, Jay's face broke out into a radiant smile. "Oh, I get it. In that case, we don't have to feel so bad. I already know his name."

Trouble at Home

Jay's father showed signs of an addictive personality early in the marriage. The first serious symptom was his excessive drinking. In their hometown of Kankakee, Illinois, population 25,000, drinking a few beers or other alcoholic beverages at a local tavern was typically the evening's entertainment. But for Jeff and Jay's dad, a few beers each night led to erratic behavior. Periods of prolonged depression resulted in frequent hospitalizations, including the use of shock treatments, all to no avail.

One bleak morning, when BJ and the boys were literally hiding from their stalking father, both boys confronted their mother. "Mom, can we divorce Daddy?" Jeff pleaded. "He scares us!"

BJ thought about it, but her options were limited. She and the boys hunkered down and tried to ride out the turmoil inside the home.

When things reached another boiling point a couple of years later, the boys approached BJ again. "Mom, can we move?" asked Jeff.

"Where would we move to?" BJ asked.

"We think we should move to California." The Golden State, a place the boys had seen only on television, appeared to be a paradise compared to the lightly populated farmlands of central Illinois.

BJ's jaw dropped. That very morning, she had been notified of an opening for a position in Covina, California, that required the experience and expertise she had developed as a health and physical education director at the local YMCA. BJ paused to wonder if God—whom she had been ignoring for years—might be reaching out to save her family from despair.

The job offer was hers, and soon mother and sons were on their way to a new life in sunny Southern California with a renewed confidence that God was directing their steps. He had provided an escape from the abusive husband and father, an ideal work environment, and a local high school with strong programs in Jay and Jeff's primary sports. All signs pointed to His Divine provision.

Life in California

With the divorce finalized and the family settled in the Covina area, Jay became the number-one doubles tennis champion for his district in high school. Both he and BJ used weight lifting to hone their strength and found this was something they could do side by side. A friendly mother-son competition would often ensue as they pushed each other to achieve their best workout. Away from the barbells, they loved dramatization and would act out skits together, applauding their own performances and laughing at their comic acts.

Upon graduation, Jeff was accepted at the University of California, San Diego (UCSD). God's opportunistic provisions continued in their lives when BJ received a call from the San Diego YMCA regarding an open position. Two weeks later, Jay and BJ were packing up to start all over again in beautiful San Diego.

Jay finished high school and began attending classes at Mira Costa College, a two-year community college. He lived with a group of friends while Jeff took up residence at UCSD.

BJ found her empty nest a lonely place. Through a singles fellowship at the local Methodist church, BJ met and ultimately married Doug Jensen, a real estate lawyer who ran a successful appraisal business. While initially wary about the new person in their mother's life, both boys came to accept this soft-spoken, calm man as their spiritual father as well as—it turned out—their employer. They both were adopted into Doug's appraisal business and found financial and personal success in this profession. Doug became a positive and encouraging force in their lives.

Dual Personality

Jay was always the life of the party; the happy-go-lucky kid who wanted everyone to feel good at the moment. When he walked into a room, there was always a huge smile when he greeted others, lighting up the faces of those he encountered. More often than not, he would swing his mother off the floor when he greeted her, which always elicited a laugh. His positive energy, sculpted physique, and his now Southern California good looks made him a candidate for a *GQ* Magazine cover. While brother Jeff considered himself a confirmed bachelor, Jay often spoke of his desire to have a family.

In private, though, Jay's life was very different. Unknown to those who loved him were his severe mood swings and encounters with depression. He didn't disclose this struggle to others but chose to suffer in silence. One girlfriend after another would break off relationships due to Jay's erratic behavior.

To the world, Jay appeared to have all he desired in life. With a reputation as the top home appraiser with Bank of America and driving a sporty BMW, he found an ideal home to rent on Coronado Island, one of the priciest enclaves in San Diego. One night during one of his desperate states of depression, however, an old high school buddy introduced Jay to crystal meth, a highly addictive recreation drug. It wasn't long before Jay was hooked on meth.

When he was high, he seemed predisposed to his father's manic-depressive disorder, and his mind and body were soon caught in the web of drug dependency. In a moment of self-awareness, though, he voluntarily admitted himself to a drug rehab program. He got some help. As he worked his way out of the horrors of drug addiction while in rehab, Jay determined he would return to school to become a counselor to others who fought the same demons.

Fatal Depression

Doug was in Los Angeles at a seminar and BJ was home alone the morning she received an alarming call from a police detective.

"I need to speak to you immediately," the detective said. "Can I come by?"

"Yes—is everything okay?" BJ asked, suddenly worried that something horrible had happened.

The detective sidestepped her question and asked for her address.

Fifteen minutes later, two uniformed men arrived at her door, identifying themselves as detectives from the San Diego Police Department. BJ held her breath as they came into her home and began questioning her about a car that was found deserted on the Coronado Bridge that links Coronado with downtown San Diego.

"Does your son drive a silver BMW convertible?"

"Yes, he does," she affirmed, worry rising in her voice.

"A car of that description was found on the Coronado Bridge, and we have reason to believe that the owner jumped to his death last evening."

BJ was stunned with disbelief.

Not Jay. He loved life. He could not have done this! There must be a mistake.

The formidable ache that pressed against her chest was unbearable. She was alone. BJ excused herself and frantically tried to contact both Doug and Jeff. Surely they would tell her that wasn't Jay on that bridge. The anesthetizing fog of grief closed in on her as her mind refused to accept the nightmare unfolding in front of her.

The police officer continued his story. BJ tried to focus, tried to listen. The detective explained that drivers crossing the bridge reported a potential jumper in 911 calls. His car was blocking the outer eastbound lane, and a man was standing next to the bridge's edge. Officers from the Coronado Police Department, which shared jurisdiction with the San Diego Police Department, were the first to arrive on the scene.

Simultaneously, an off-duty San Diego police officer who had heard the 911 call stopped to assist. The Coronado officers were talking to Jay, trying to coax him to reconsider jumping from the bridge. Jay was standing next to the concrete edge, between the counseling voices from Coronado and the approaching figure of the San Diego police officer, who continued to move toward Jay. Suddenly, the San Diego officer broke into a run to tackle Jay and stop him from jumping.

Jay, an athlete whose instinct was never to be tackled, pressed his palms on the edge and leapt to his death over the side of the bridge.

He fell 200 feet before he hit the water.

Introspection

Gray days of despair enshrouded BJ, Doug, and Jeff, who were unaware that a San Diego police officer had attempted to stop Jay from jumping over the edge. Instead, questions kept replaying in their minds:

What could we have done differently?

Why didn't we suspect something was amiss?

What was the trigger that prompted Jay to think about ending his life?

What clues did Jay leave behind?

No answers were forthcoming, and the bleak days continued. Doug's parents made the arrangements for a memorial service. Friends generously brought in food for everyone who gathered at the home to pray and help manage day-to-day necessities.

For weeks BJ was unable to eat. She would come to the table only to burst out crying and run to the solace of her bed. Doug would hold her for hours as she anguished. As horrendous a time as this was, BJ tells of the invisible arms she felt warming her cold body as she leaned into God's promises of comfort.

A mother's heart cannot contain the despair that comes with the loss of a child. A suicide multiplies the feelings of deprivation. No words of comfort or promise that God can heal the brokenhearted can assuage the darkness that surrounds the visions, the questions, and the unrelenting reality that one's child has taken his own life. BJ would sometimes argue with the Holy Spirit about the whys and wonders of such a senseless loss. She found herself compelled to go to a private place and sit in silence, just as she had as a child. She felt God's pervasive love surrounding her as she called upon His strength to defeat death's victory.

An Unplanned Meeting

BJ awoke one morning several months after the funeral, determined to take a step of healing. She set off from her San Diego home to drive over the Coronado Bridge with Jay's dog Cabo, a Siberian Husky. Once in Coronado, they'd go for a walk on the beach. She slipped on old comfortable sweats, hardly bothering to brush her hair. Then she steeled herself for what was to come.

That first drive over the bridge was excruciating. BJ cried and cried, trying to keep her eyes focused on the road and not toward the fatal edge. She knew she needed to drive it alone. The unnerving cry of Cabo, anticipating a return home to Jay, brought more unbearable pain.

The two walked back and forth along the sandy beach, calmed by the steady waves. BJ was discovering that time alone with the Lord was a time her heart would fill with old hymns she had heard as a child. She hummed her favorite song of trusting the faithfulness of God, morning by morning bringing His mercies to her.

As she climbed back into her car with sandy feet and a windswept appearance, she felt an urge to stop by the Coronado Police Department offices. *There's never any parking on these streets*, she reminded herself, so she thought about forgetting her idea. But as she approached the station, a parking spot opened up right in front of the main door.

"What am I doing here?" she muttered to herself. "I'm a mess. What do I expect to hear? These men probably don't even know about Jay's case." Nonetheless, she exited the car and walked to the front desk.

"Hi. Sorry to bother you. I'm the mother of the man that

jumped off the bridge . . . ."

BJ almost turned to leave as she could not finish the sentence she had begun.

"Wait!" said the uniformed officer behind the desk. "Can I help?"

"I'm not sure why I'm here," BJ answered.-

"Well, we've kind of been expecting you. We thought you might have questions about the incident. Come on in the back room."

The officer put a report in her hands.

"Can I take a look?"

"Yes, I would like you to see it."

To BJ, it seemed as if the officer wanted her to know something, but she didn't know what questions to ask.

She scanned the report, then listened to the officer explain that territorial disputes often came up between the San Diego and Coronado police departments with respect to accidents and other incidents on the bridge. While his team was attempting to take control the night of Jay's suicide that night, their attempts to calm Jay were thwarted when the San Diego officer crouched and sprinted toward him from the other side.

"Our training counsels us not to aggravate the potential jumper, but to coax and relax and otherwise distract the individual from thoughts of suicide. We believe more departments should have consistent training for these delicate encounters," he said.

She returned the report to the officer, hugging him as tears came to her eyes. What could BJ do to be sure this would never happen to another mother due to a lack of suicide prevention training?

BJ was convinced that she could be used to bring good out of a tragedy if she were willing to challenge the system. Her first step was seek out an attorney friend and have him file a lawsuit against the City of San Diego and the San Diego Police Department.

After eighteen months of negotiations, BJ dropped the suit when the city demonstrated that they had formulated the first program in the nation to provide trained mental health professionals to work alongside officers for cases such as potential suicides. The program was titled PERT, or the Psychiatric Emergency Response Team. The *San Diego Union-Tribune's* headline on their website read: "Program is the first in the nation. Psychologists join cops on patrol."

No mention was made of Jay Morgan's death or the Jensens' resolute battle to prevent another mishap by the officers commissioned to protect and serve the public.

And that was perfectly fine with BJ.

A Surprise Encounter

A few years later, speaking at a woman's conference in San Diego, BJ was embraced by a woman who confessed that if it weren't for the PERT program, she wouldn't be getting married the following June.

When BJ asked how that was possible, the woman said her fiancé had threatened to jump from a structure but was talked down by a police psychologist from PERT. Her fiancé was put under a doctor's care and prescribed the appropriate medications to balance his depression.

BJ stood in silence as the woman walked away. *Well, Lord,* she sighed in her heart. *You saved that one, and many more, because Your*

Spirit directed me and I listened and obeyed. This is Your love note to me, and I am grateful.

Within her church, BJ found solace serving alongside the choir by signing the words to the hymns for the benefit of the deaf and hard of hearing in the congregation. When initially asked by the choir director to perform the sign language, she was hesitant. But BJ listened and knew God was asking her to be His vessel and demonstrate what a love relationship with Him actually looks like.

Others, young and old, became interested and soon the silent "Love in Motion Choir" was signing hymns and choruses in various churches around San Diego. The choir drew national attention, which is why BJ found herself in Washington D.C. at the Compassionate Friends national conference.

BJ stood before her choir in silence as she dedicated this performance to Jay's memory. She had selected two poignant pieces for their finale: Lee Ann Womack's "I Hope You Dance," and Josh Groban's "To Where You Are," in which the final lyrics portray the hope of heaven:

Are you gently sleeping
Here inside my dream
And isn't faith believing
All power can't be seen.
As my heart holds you
Just one beat away
I cherish all you gave me everyday

'Cause you are my

Forever love
Watching me from up above
And I believe
That angels breathe
And that love will live on and never leave . . .

The audience was effusive as they gave the choir a standing ovation. Approaching BJ from the side of the room was a rather tall gentleman whose eyes were filled with tears but his face was smiling.

"You've given me a love note from God!" he exclaimed, clasping BJ's hands in his. "My daughter passed away recently, and I've been asking God where He was during all of this pain and grief. I came to this conference looking for Him. The last two songs you sang were her favorites, and we played them at her funeral."

BJ thanked the man for his praise, but he had one more item to share.

"The other thing I wanted to tell you is that my daughter's name was Morgan, and your son's last name was Morgan. I believe with all my heart our Lord wanted us to know that our Morgans are dancing together in heaven. My soul is quieted and at peace."

BJ choked back tears, knowing that God's signature was on this precious moment.

The crushing blows of this life can leave us broken and bitter, or they can leave us believing and better. Every misstep can be used by the Creator to equip us for a mission, if only to break the power of evil that wants to claim death as its victory. The hope of the reunion of God's saints in heaven can slowly clear away the fog of grief, gradually lift your countenance and regenerate your heart with peace. BJ's story demonstrates the power of God's Spirit to minister in concrete ways—if we open our hearts to hear His direction. His signs and songs of healing will permeate our lives if we will look up and receive.

"May the favor of the Lord our God rest upon us; establish the work of our hands for us—yes, establish the work of our hands."

—Psalm 90:17 (NIV)

Thoughts to Ponder

- Is there a time each day when you might sit in silence to hear God's voice? Ask His Holy Spirit to enter in and give you understanding.

- Can you make something better in the memory of your child? At the school, in the hospital, in adopting heightened safety guidelines for children?

- Order a CD of Christian praise-and-worship music or download songs to your mp3 player. Seek out the lyrics and let them minister to your heart.

About the Mother: BJ Jensen

To BJ Jensen, Jay will always remain in her mind as the same outgoing, intelligent, and talented boy, a joy to raise and a young man that made her proud.

BJ's story builds upon her capacity to listen in silence and act on the guidance of the Holy Spirit that led her through challenging times in her life. While she argued with the still small voice of God's wisdom, it was His power that lifted her out of the desolation of her son's death. Through incredible coincidences and life-changing outcomes, other young lives have been saved.

Life took on a new perspective for Jay's brother, Jeff, following the suicide. He is now happily married and the father of three children. After Jay's death, Doug went on to earn his doctorate in Biblical Studies and Biblical Counseling so that he could help other families not only survive but thrive through tragic life experiences.

Together, Doug and BJ serve their community and travel internationally as counselors and worship presenters to other grieving families. In May 2011, they completed their co-authored book, *Finding Hope After the Devastating Loss of Beloved Children*, sharing their insights and walking hurting parents through the stages of grief following the death of a child.

11

In Service to Our Country

Military Honoring Inspires Outreach to Others

Kenny Necochea was an incredibly likable kid growing up in the San Diego area. Although shy like his mother, Donna, his easygoing, humble nature earned him lasting friendships in childhood.

His nature was that of family peacemaker because Kenny grew up in a blended family when his mom married Neal Wright following a divorce. But he could also be goofy and make everyone laugh. He was protective of his stepbrother, Dylan, who was eleven years younger, and seldom had a word of criticism for anyone.

When Kenny was in grade school, Donna recognized their son's unique talents were not necessarily found in the classroom. Kenny was a good musician and artist. While not aggressively competitive, he liked to challenge himself. Golf offered the individual competition that appealed to Kenny—and he was a natural from tee to green. Off the golf course, his knack for assembling complex parts into an integral whole meant he could be counted upon at Christmastime to construct Dylan's new stroller or put together his toys.

As he grew older, Kenny's continued interest in construction and welding blossomed into a hobby of designing and building competitive go-carts. Kenny's grandfather, William Gilmore, a retired electrician, became Kenny's "crew chief" as they set out to compete in local go-cart races. Grandpa Gilmore's trailer contained all the spare parts and tools necessary for quick repairs at the race sites. Kenny loved racing and outgunning his opponents to the checkered flag. He was respected by his competitors in an arena where he excelled.

After high school, Kenny worked on the maintenance crew at Horizon Christian School, where he had been a student. His job gave him the flexibility to mentor and coach students who needed a big brother to guide them. Not interested in attending a traditional four-year college at the time, Kenny enrolled in an Emergency Medical Technician (EMT) course with the thought of becoming a fireman.

Soon after beginning the course, though, Kenny contracted mononucleosis. This caused him to miss classes, which resulted in an automatic failure. Kenny's illness and subsequent lack of direction brought on depression and confusion about his future.

Boot Camp

It was Grandpa Gilmore, a former U.S. Army captain, who encouraged Kenny to consider the military, where he could receive training and possibly earn a college degree. A Navy recruiter inspired Kenny to bring home an application. The Navy seemed safer to Kenny than the Marines, and he had the idea that he might be able to train as an underwater welder. After sleeping on his decision, Kenny determined that being cooped up on a ship didn't suit him, so he changed his mind and joined the Army the next day.

He wanted to become an infantryman. "God is leading me," he told his grandfather. "I want to make a difference."

Kenny's Basic Combat Training (BCT or "boot camp"), along with his Advanced Individual Training, were conducted at Fort Benning, Georgia. During four winter months, in sleet and snow, he and his army buddies were molded into the men and women who make our military strong. The focus was to tear down weaknesses and build up strengths.

While complaining to his mother about frozen toes and bugs in his boots, Kenny carried on, earning the respect of his commanders. On Sunday nights, Kenny's mom, stepdad, and stepbrother flooded him with support, each writing separate letters of encouragement and tucking them in with his favorite goodies to make a weekly care package. Kenny responded well to the Army's regimen. He had left home a typical twenty-year-old sloppy boy and had developed into a strong, confident, well-organized man.

After boot camp, Kenny's squadron was sent to Fort Campbell, a complete military city within the city of Clarksville, Kentucky. It was here, as they continued training against al Qaeda tactics, that the soldiers would wait for their orders to the Middle East. The danger awaiting them was not sugarcoated. They were drilled to be ready for anything.

Meeting Someone Special

While Kenny always had a number of girlfriends, he hadn't been in a serious relationship until a friend in his squadron introduced him to Laura. When Kenny was awarded leave so he could visit his family in San Diego prior to his deployment, he decided to bring Laura along so she could meet his family. During the visit, however, Laura suffered a mild stroke, which led to the discovery of a small hole in her heart. When his leave was over, Kenny had to return to Clarksville to prepare for his deployment. Laura remained for a time with Donna and Neal in the care of San Diego medical specialists.

Donna offered to help bring Laura back to her home in Kentucky and also arranged to have a pre-deployment visit with Kenny. They knew time was short. The Army provided a hotel room on the grounds where Donna and Kenny "bunked" together. They shared a time of laughter and closeness, and she met the buddies that Kenny had spoken of so highly. Putting faces with names helped.

They also explored the area around Clarksville, venturing out to the Cumberland Caverns, a remarkable feat of nature discovered in the 1800s. One room within the thirty-two miles of coves was called the "Ten Acre Room" due to the expansiveness of the cavern.

The last night before her departure, Donna hosted a dinner for Kenny and his friends at a local restaurant. They laughed together as Kenny acknowledged he had never pictured himself drinking in a bar with his mother. Donna sat back in her chair, admiring the young men sharing the evening with her. *These are the finest of their generation*, she thought. *They are polite, well trained men, ready to serve our country at war.*

Three days later, on June 6, 2010, the 2nd Brigade of the 502nd Infantry Regiment left for Afghanistan. They were among the 30,000 troops transported to the Middle East as part of a surge effort known as Operation Enduring Freedom.

Fighting Season

Summer is fighting season in Afghanistan. Deployed to Kandahar, the country's second largest city, the 502nd's campaign was to pacify the surrounding countryside, a crucial swath of southern Afghanistan known as the birthplace of the Taliban. The insurgents were funneling fighters, drugs, and explosives into the area to stage attacks on small villages, thereby forcing inhabitants to join their forces or flee to the surrounding desert until American troops could reclaim the towns.

Success in Kandahar, it was believed, would lead to overall victory given that the Taliban's power base was rooted in this region. Kenny's combat team breached and held a strategic area of land that Taliban fighters had dominated for years. "We are on the front lines," Kenny commented in a Facebook entry. "We are dealing with evil head on!"

Kenny had a heart for the homeless children who wandered the village streets. He studied their language, Pashto, and became a translator for his command. The children would laugh at Kenny's Pashtun expressions spoken with an American accent. Offering crayons, candy, and fresh water, he befriended many of the children with his sincere attention, even though the Taliban used children to infiltrate and destroy American camps. Children here were considered potential threats.

His sergeant would often inquire where all the bottled water was going, knowing that Kenny was hydrating a population of needy children. Kenny's engaging manner and humorous attempts to speak their language, as well as his peace offerings, created mutually trusting friendships with the village children. Another of Kenny's Facebook entries stated, "The Taliban forcefully remove them from their homes. We restore peace to their lives by returning them to their homes . . . seeing their smiling faces and accepting the gestures of thanks is all the reward I need."

Within the brigade, facing danger *shonna ba shonna* (shoulder to shoulder) engendered camaraderie. Nicknames were a common bond of friendship. Kenny was "Neco," derived from his last name,

Necochea. Danny Morneault became "Frenchy." Christopher Sullivan was shortened to "Sully." Given names were forgotten as the nicknames confirmed the sense of family within the squadron.

Don't Let Mom See This!

One night in the barracks when everyone was in their bunks talking, laughing, reading, or writing, Kenny observed the different personalities among his buddies. He wrote this: "These people understand each other. We accept each other. They are brave souls. We are seeing life and death every day, and I know all of us will not return home. Whatever my Savior decides for me, I'm completely fine with it."

Kenny's journal contained the realities of war. He chatted on Facebook with Neal, relating an incident on patrol where he looked to the ground and was amazed to see that he was standing on an IED (improvised explosive device) that failed to explode. "Don't let Mom see this," he pleaded.

His mother kept her computer open to Facebook every day at work, hoping for an update from Kenny. She didn't realize that no news could be the best news.

There were agonizing stretches where he wouldn't post anything for a week. Phone calls were just as sporadic; they never knew when Kenny would call, which was often in the middle of the night in San Diego but the middle of the day in Afghanistan.

Kenny's mechanical expertise, which he had developed while racing and working on go-carts with his grandfather, served his unit well in Afghanistan. He was meticulous at loading trucks for balance and safety. Kenny's skill in maneuvering large equipment through potentially mined fields brought him the respect of his commander and facilitated the success of the "Strike Brigade" in flushing out Taliban fighters in areas that no U.S. conventional force had previously occupied. Kenny was the handpicked driver, always successful in avoiding dangerous situations and ensuring the equipment was prepared and ready.

Trusting an Informer

It was early in the morning on December 12, 2010, when a minivan approached the checkpoint on the outskirts of the army base. The guards recognized the familiar face of an Afghan man they had come to trust as a reliable resource for information. The van approached the barrier at a normal speed.

Suddenly accelerating, the van crashed through the gate, heading directly toward the barracks where Kenny and others were still sleeping in their bunks. Frenchy, positioned on the roof of the barracks, caught sight of the speeding van. Considering it a potential threat, he drew his rifle, expecting to hear a siren alert or signal to fire upon the approaching vehicle. But within seconds the van, loaded with a thousand pounds of explosives, careened into the barracks. A massive explosion destroyed the concrete structure, leaving a mass of debris and dust.

Kenny did not survive the suicide bombing. In a split second, the impact took his life while he slept, as well as the lives of four other soldiers inside the destroyed barracks. Kenny and his comrades left this earth without fear, pain, or even awareness that time among the living had passed.

The Return Home

On a Sunday afternoon in December, Neal Wright was returning home from a charity motorcycle ride benefiting homeless men and women in San Diego County.

Just before entering the house, Neal noticed two men in military attire exiting a car parked in front of his home. Neal's wife, Donna, was working in their home office. Their ten-year-old son, Dylan, pulled aside the blinds and observed two men walking toward their house. He called out, "Hey Mom, there are two army guys coming to our front door!"

At precisely the same moment, Neal and Donna knew that they would soon be the recipients of horrible news. They were sadly correct. The military officers formally told them that their son, Kenny Necochea, had been killed while defending lives in Afghanistan. In a flash, this family was changed forever.

Hearing the knock at the door, followed by the conciliatory words, "We regret to inform you . . ." seemed like a bad dream. The past they remembered and the future they had hoped for were shattered by the news of Kenny's death.

Donna and Neal, consumed by grief, listened to the protocol for bringing Kenny home. The next morning they were flown to Dover Air Force Base in Delaware and escorted with great dignity to Fisher House for Families of the Fallen, a facility designed to provide short-term, on-base lodging to families who travel to Dover to witness the arrival of their deceased loved ones. Joining the ranks of Gold Star families is never a choice, but an honor bestowed upon those parents who have suffered the loss of their son or daughter in service to their country.

A funded credit card was provided for their needs during their stay. The utmost care and respect was shown as they left their belongings and boarded a bus, along with several other similarly stricken families, to be transported to the airfield.

At midnight, the families found themselves standing on a frozen tarmac awaiting their children's dignified transfer back to American soil. One by one, eight caskets, each draped with an American flag, were carried off the plane. Five of the young men had died alongside Kenny; two others died in separate incidents in the same area.

"It was horrible," said Donna about the experience. "We couldn't move toward Kenny or touch the casket. I wanted to run to him and walk alongside him."

Freezing from the December wind, the families stood in place as directed. Donna was wracked by uncontrollable sobs—the woeful sounds of a brokenhearted mother.

Angel Flight

Several dignitaries and high-ranking officers were present on that freezing night to offer condolences and share their heartfelt regret to the despairing families. Protocol dictates that the bodies of deceased soldiers are not to be touched or seen until autopsies can be performed on American soil.

The next step was to transfer the bodies to a U.S. Air Force Base in the vicinity of their home. Kenny's "Angel Flight" was by private jet from Dover to Marine Corps Air Station Miramar in San Diego. There, family and friends as well as Donna and Neal's pastor, Mike MacIntosh of Horizon Christian Fellowship, awaited his arrival.

The Patriot Guard Riders (PGR) also stood at attention on the tarmac at MCAS Miramar. This diverse amalgamation of motorcyclists from across the country comprises a patriotic all-volunteer honor guard formed to ensure dignity and respect at memorial services honoring fallen military heroes, first responders, and honorably discharged veterans. Their purpose is to shield the mourning family from potential interruptions by protestors and to fulfill their motto "Standing for Those Who Stood for Us."

As Kenny's flag-draped casket was carried from the plane, the PGR formed a pathway from the plane to the hearse and, from there, escorted Kenny's body to the funeral home. Their presence at Miramar and at the final burial and military ceremony at Fort Rosecrans caused Donna and Neal to realize that the life and death of their son was honored and valued by their fellow Americans.

A Final Dining Room Encounter

The Wrights received numerous cards, letters, books, flowers, and plants from family and friends as well as from people they didn't know. Their dining room table became a display area for this outpouring of love. Kenny's medals, photos, and other mementos filled the table, keeping his memory alive in the darkness of the family's overwhelming grief.

Following the burial, Neal and Donna held each other through the night as the crushing pain of Kenny's death brought a flood of tears. In the early morning hours, their home security alarm suddenly started blaring. The alarm monitor read *Dining Room Door*. While Donna jumped out of her warm bed to turn off the alarm, Neal rushed to the dining room, fearing someone might have absconded with Kenny's medals.

As Donna came into the dining room, a sense of unexplainable calm flooded over her. Her fear evaporated. "It was as if Kenny was hugging me, letting me know it was okay; he was fine and in a very good, safe, loving, beautiful place." Both Donna and Neal returned to bed experiencing a tangible comfort that allowed them to rest with a sense of peace.

Their security alarm hasn't gone off since that night.

Thoughts to Ponder

- Consider an area of service that might commemorate your child's life.

- Are there mementos that you might accumulate in a scrapbook or collage to honor the life of your child?

- Were there any unexplainable events that brought a moment of comfort to your time of grieving? Open a journal and relate the account of that experience. Consider that God uses His incredible power to reach out to us in ways we can only describe as miraculous.

About the Mother: Donna Wright

Reaching out together, Donna and Neal volunteer for the Wounded Warrior Foundation. When a story hits the news of American casualties, or when there is a call to honor the loss of a local military man or woman, the Wrights cling to the unconditional comfort they received in the knowledge that the Lord of this life and the life beyond has joined these heroes together in a place where they will serve together, without pain or suffering, for eternity.

Since the celebration of Kenny's life and death, Neal has ridden with the Patriot Guard Riders and has had the privilege of meeting many Gold Star parents who have suffered the same loss as the Wrights. Although his time with grieving parents is a painful reminder of Kenny's loss, Neal always offers his witness that the memory of one's fallen son or daughter lives on in the life of those who experience the loss.

12

Under God's Umbrella

Ministry to Other Mothers is a Testimony to Son's Life

If you were to ask those who knew them well, Daisy and Dick Catchings' marriage was made in heaven. They grew up knowing each other, attending the same schools but separated by three years. When Dick graduated from high school, he joined the U.S. Army. Daisy, vivacious and fun to be around, enjoyed her junior and senior years of high school while Dick served our country.

A few weeks after graduating, she was hanging out at the Hub Club, a local gathering place where teens met for dancing. That evening, Dick dropped in after his discharge from military service.

It was love at first sight, as Daisy will quickly tell you. She was seventeen years old, Dick twenty, but she knew he was the love of her life. They began dating in July and were married in December. Although her parents were disappointed their daughter was forgoing college, it was apparent these two were committed to each other. Daisy became Mrs. Richard Catchings on one of the happiest days of her life.

The joy of their marriage included having a family. After three years of anticipation, the couple learned Daisy was pregnant. Little did they know this baby would prove to be a miracle. When she was eight months along, Daisy began hemorrhaging, causing their son Danny to come into the world ahead of schedule. Upon later examination, Daisy was diagnosed with endometriosis, a female health disorder that occurs when cells from the lining of the uterus grow in other areas of the body. This condition leads to irregular bleeding and problems getting pregnant. There would be just one child, this special son, in the Catchings family.

Daisy and Dick were working parents as Danny hit the preschool years. Unusual in today's world, Danny's preschool teacher—in a public school—demonstrated the importance of acknowledging God in their lives by leading the class in saying grace before dismissing her hungry charges to eat lunch inside the cafeteria. Danny loved the daily ritual of saying grace each day at school.

One evening as Daisy placed the evening meal in front of her family, Danny folded his little hands and bowed his head. This had not been the practice in their home since his parents were not churchgoers. But that evening, when Danny thanked the Lord for the special dinner and for the mommy who cooked it for him—and finished with an enthusiastic "Amen!"—something happened.

Daisy looked at Dick with a tear in her eye. "Well," she said, "I guess it takes a four-year-old to wake us up to God's grace in our life."

Dick smiled and nodded. *"Out of the mouths of babes . . ."*

From that day forward, no meal was enjoyed without the family first thanking God for His provision. And every Sunday, the Catchings family could be found in their local church. Soon their lives were committed to serving God. In the months and years that followed, there were many times when Daisy and Dick expressed their appreciation to their son for bringing them to the Lord.

Danny the Athlete

Like his father, Danny was an extraordinary athlete. Sports were his world, and academics weren't even a strong second. A tall, blond, handsome young man, Danny participated in basketball, tennis, and golf throughout high school. When he was offered a basketball scholarship to Fresno Pacific University, Danny readily accepted and immediately doubled his workout schedule to be ready for college ball in the Central California city of Fresno.

The college scene pulled Danny away from church, but God had other plans for him. Being a star athlete drew the attention of a local church pastor, who approached Danny and asked if he would be interested in coaching the youth basketball team. At the outset, this was just a fun job opportunity for Danny, but his heart was soon touched by the needs of the kids he coached.

Being part of a growing youth program rekindled Danny's interest in having a closer relationship with God. He viewed coaching basketball as an opportunity to teach his players about the importance of good sportsmanship, the power of prayer, and the love of physical activity to maintain the healthy body God had provided.

As Danny left college, he chose to become a full-time youth pastor, drawing many young people to church and pointing a new path toward God and away from worldly pursuits. Danny loved to sing, and his guitar-playing fests drew young people into a church they might never have attended otherwise.

This was his calling in his twenties. Danny was singing to the Lord a new song, running defense against the drugs and alcohol that trapped many young people in the community.

Eventually, Danny came home to live with Dick and Daisy, continuing to work as a youth pastor in their local church. One time, while playing an energetic game of volleyball with the kids, Danny twisted his ankle and broke his foot, ending up in a cast for several weeks.

Meanwhile, he'd taken interest in a wonderful young woman, and he was thinking that she could be the one.

Late for a Meeting

After returning from an evening out, Danny stood at the foot of his parents' bed, relating the events of the day and complaining about the cast around his broken foot. "I'm going to see if the doctor can take this thing off tomorrow. I know it's healed. The itching is driving me crazy," Danny said to his folks.

"Don't rush it!" said Daisy. "Be patient. Get to bed and have a good night's sleep. Love you."

"Love you guys," he said over his shoulder as he left their bedroom.

The next morning, Dick had just arrived home after an early morning tennis game and Daisy was at work. Their church pastor called around 9:30 a.m.

"Dick, where's Danny? He was due here for a nine o'clock meeting, and he's never late," the pastor said.

"Gosh, I have no idea," Dick replied. "Both Daisy and I left early. Let me call her and see what she says."

Dick reached Daisy at the office and told her that Danny had missed his 9 a.m. appointment at church.

"Maybe he overslept," she offered.

"I'll check his bedroom."

He tapped a couple of times on the bedroom door. When there was no answer, he gently pushed open the door and saw Danny was still sleeping.

Dick walked in, telling Danny that he was late for a meeting at church. As he drew closer to the bed, he noticed that Danny had not stirred when he walked in or when he spoke to him.

Dick took a closer look—and saw that Danny was no longer breathing. He touched his shoulder and received no response, then touched the skin on his face. It was cold.

Danny had gone to be with the Lord.

Dick immediately ran back to the kitchen to call 911, but there was nothing medically that could be done. Sometime during the night, Danny had suffered a major heart attack. At the age of twenty-eight, Danny was gone.

Daisy rushed home from the office to the sight that no mother should ever see—paramedics using defibrillators on her son's chest to shock the heart into restarting.

An autopsy would reveal that Danny's death from a massive cardiomyopathy event was instantaneous, and neither she nor Dick could have done anything to prevent his death—even if they had witnessed the heart attack. Time of death was estimated to be at 4 a.m.

One moment, all was well in Daisy's world. She woke up on a sunny day and left for work thinking about what she would prepare for dinner that night. Just a few hours later, though, her world collapsed when the inconceivable happened.

Daisy and Dick prayed together that the God they loved would sustain them, lift them, and carry them through the terrible pain in their broken hearts.

In the days and weeks that would follow, the real meaning of the word *church* was demonstrated to Dick and Daisy. Their church family blanketed them with gentle support, guiding them through the decisions that filled their days. Danny's memorial service would be filled with his music, and his heart for the Lord would be preached.

Before the service, Dick sat weeping with their pastor. "Why didn't God take me?" he asked. "I've lived a full life. His whole life was ahead of him."

The pastor put his hand on Dick's shoulder. "Dick, I imagine that is what Danny is asking the Lord right now. 'Lord? My dad and mom deserve to be in this glorious place. Why didn't you bring them instead of me?'"

Dick managed a faint smile. Trusting God's plan would be important in the days ahead.

The memorial service was filled with young and old who came to honor Danny's life as well as the parents who raised him. God was faithful to His promise to bring good out of all circumstances. At the end of the service, which included an invitation to get right with God, twenty-six young people gave their lives to Christ. The seeds sown from Danny's outreach in life were fruitful and harvested in his death. The void of his death remained to be filled, but his purpose in living was achieved.

Sleepless Nights Turned into Conversations

Daisy didn't sleep very well for months following her son's death. She needed to talk with Danny, having the conversations she had so treasured with him. She remembered how Danny would say to her and Dick, "Now that you've *s'plained* it this way. . . " when they gave him guidance. She recalled how Danny would show his enthusiasm for her cooking by exclaiming, "This is deeelicious!"

So precious were these memories that she wanted to capture them on paper. She began to fill the sleepless hours in her nights by writing letters to Danny. She reminded him of their adventures. She asked him about heaven. She told him how difficult life was without him. Then she wrote letters as if Danny were replying to her—letters of encouragement, of letting go, of scriptural descriptions of heaven.

Slowly, Daisy's heart began to mend. Sleepless nights transformed into rested mornings. After some time, these letters were carefully boxed and stored away in the garage.

One of Daisy's writings contained a transcript of Danny's appearance on a Christian radio station in Los Angeles. She had recorded the thirty-minute talk that he gave about the story of Elijah, who challenged 450 prophets in the land of Samaria to give up their false god, Baal. Elijah proposed a test between God and the idol Baal: the 450 prophets of Baal and Elijah would each lay a bull over an altar made up of wood and then pray to their God to rain down fire and consume the animal sacrifice. The Baal prophets prayed, and nothing happened. When Elijah prayed to the one true God, fire rained down from heaven, consuming his sacrifice— which had been doused with water beforehand.

Danny noted that those who worshipped Baal were discouraged because they could no longer find satisfaction in a powerless god that didn't exist. "We see this today—people all over the world serving their own Baal, gods they believe they can find in narcotics and in bottles," he said on the radio. "And they're discouraged because of their lack of faith in the one true God. Elijah had so much faith—the kind of faith you and I must have."

Then Danny read from 1 Kings 18:38-9 (NIV): "Then the fire of the Lord fell and burned up the sacrifice, the wood, the stones and the soil, and also licked up the water in the trench. When all the people saw this, they fell prostrate and cried, "The Lord—he is God! The Lord—he is God!"

The people fell upon their faces. They worshipped God, Danny noted. Yet even after that powerful fire from heaven, acknowledging the one true God, Elijah became discouraged. He traveled into the wilderness, asking God to take his life.

"Is this Elijah?" Danny asked his audience. "A great man of God suddenly filled with self-pity . . . Elijah was tired, there was a famine and he must have been hungry, and he'd been through an emotional experience. These are the circumstances Satan uses to bring discouragement into our lives. But God was faithful. He sent angels to Elijah with food and water. He let Elijah sleep. He strengthened him for another mission. And yet, Elijah was still discouraged."

Danny concluded his message with the story of a skipper who was putting his small craft out to sea in the Gulf of Mexico. Warned of imminent danger by friends and jeered by those who gathered to see him off in his rickety boat, the skipper told the crowd, "I have a date with the Gulf Stream." This wise skipper knew he would not be sailing under the momentum of his engines. He had a date with a power greater than himself or his small boat—a river of current that would take him to the Florida peninsula.

"So did Elijah. So do you," concluded Danny. "If your life is chopping in a sea of discouragement, then you have a date with the Gulf Stream—God Himself!"

Encouragement Turns into a National Ministry

That message of encouragement, in Danny's own words and voice, recorded before his journey to heaven, cast a life-saving buoy for Daisy and Dick to cling to when discouragement crept into their lives. They knew that rest, proper diet, and talking to the Lord were proven physical provisions they needed. The power generated from the One True Source of comfort inspired Daisy to recognize that God was strengthening her for a new mission of bringing His hope of healing to other mothers whose children had died.

One day, Daisy retrieved the boxes from the garage and used her letters to Danny as the basis for a book she entitled, *Under God's Umbrella*. A dear friend, Donna Luke, was a huge help in publishing the book, which touched a deep need in the Christian community.

After the book was printed, Umbrella Ministries was launched and grew into a national ministry bringing " . . . the Father of all compassion and the God of all comfort, who comforts us in all our troubles, so that we can comfort those in any trouble with the comfort we ourselves receive from God" (2 Corinthians 1:3-4, NIV). This foundational verse describes perfectly the mother-to-mother ministry Umbrella Ministries offers, encouraging grieving mothers and providing a link to a brighter future from the depths of despair.

In the prelude to her book, Daisy writes: "No, you never get over the loss. Yes, the pain and tears return at the most unexpected times. But you will also experience joy, laughter, and a greater walk with God. As the storms of life come crashing down around us, we stand strong, firm, and confident under God's umbrella."

Grieving the death of a child can be a painful and lonely struggle, and working through the horrible anguish requires tremendous effort, patience, faith, and hope. Ever since Daisy lost Danny she has been offering respite, holding God's umbrella over those who need hope and encouragement to take one more step through the valley of the shadow of death.

Thoughts to Ponder

- Consider writing a letter to your child. Recall fond memories, special celebrations, and tributes or accolades your child received. Tell your child about what's happening in your life today, about the void that is ever-present, and the new things that have occurred. Keep a journal of your letters.

- Helping another person can be part of the journey of healing. When you are able, reach out to another mother you know whose child has died. Send a note of understanding or take a gift or food to the family. Offer to walk together or have a cup of coffee one Saturday.

- Go to www.umbrellaministries.com to learn if there is a branch of Umbrella Ministries in your area. Find out about Bible studies, craft ideas, and get synopses of conference presentations. If you need support, contact the website.

About the Mother: Daisy Catchings-Shader

Daisy Catchings-Shader serves as the director of Umbrella Ministries, a nonprofit organization for mothers who have suffered the loss of a child. Umbrella Ministries presents "Journey of the

Heart" conferences throughout the United States—a special time for mothers to give and receive comfort from one another and benefit from those who are walking on the same road in a journey toward healing.

Daisy is an inspirational and motivational speaker, author, and member of the Christian Writers Guild. She currently serves on the board of Women's Ministries at Southwest Community Church in Indian Wells, California. Several years after her husband's death, Daisy married Dave Shader.

Please visit the main website for Umbrella Ministries at www.umbrellaministries.org. The website provides information on ministries in the United States and dates and times for various programs and conferences.

A Final Word

By Pastor Mike MacIntosh

When I wrote my book ***When Your World Falls Apart: Life Lessons from a Ground Zero Chaplain,*** I was reaching out to every individual who has had a life crushing 9/11 experience. The world grieved for the families and personnel who died and survived that horrific day. There was an outpouring of love and support for those whose lives were crushed by an act of terror. It has been my prayer to bring the lessons of those losses to those whose lives are forever changed by the death of a loved one yet find themselves alone and lost in their devastation.

Hope for a Broken Heart has the same goal of encouragement. Twelve stories of mothers journeying from loss to legacy demonstrate the power of God's hand touching lives in miraculous ways. While only the "major" catastrophes make the news, there are thousands of families and friends whose worlds have fallen apart, desperate to know how to get back to life. Like the familiar nursery rhyme Humpty Dumpty, "all the king's horses and all the king's men" can't put their lives back together again. In each mother's story there is the acknowledgement that looking up to the God of all comfort would bring them through the debilitating, dark valley of the shadow of death.

Are you in that valley today? Did you find in each chapter God-coincidences that showed Him at work in each of their lives? Go back to the marks you made in the margin when you saw God-moments in each mother's life. Return to the Points to Ponder and work through the healing suggestions, a day at a time.

An Important Decision

There is another important decision you can make for your life today. Jesus tells us in the Bible that we can come into a personal relationship with God our Father by asking Him into our lives. Remember the author's little boy, Jeff, who put his little hands over his heart and joyfully told his mother that he had invited Jesus to enter into his life. Could that be your decision today? Would you like the God of all creation to live within you and provide the comfort and direction that the twelve mothers in this book found? Your life will be changed forever if you pray this simple prayer with me right now, wherever you are, by simply saying,

"Father, I know I need you in my life. I cannot survive this ground zero loss without you. Please forgive me the sins of my life. Jesus, I ask you now to enter into my heart, forever walk with me and bring me the hope for today and the promise of eternity with you. I ask this in Jesus's name. Amen"

Today you are born anew. Your life will never be the same because you now have the power of the Holy Spirit directing, comforting, bringing life and light into every day. Will there be struggles? Of course. Will there be detours? Yes there will. But you will never be alone in those struggles. You have the ultimate Hope for a Broken Heart. Praising God for your decision.

— Pastor Mike MacIntosh

* * * * *

Mike MacIntosh is the Pastor at Horizon Christian Fellowship, San Diego, California, as well as a chaplain specializing in Critical

Incident Stress Management. Drawing on over thirty years of pastoral and counseling experience, as well as some painful passages of his own life, Mike speaks to congregations around the world, offering God's forgiveness and mercy. As a member of a National Disaster Response Team, Mike was on call for the month of September, 2001 and spent several weeks ministering to rescue personnel at the site of the World Trade Center disaster. Visit www. hcf.org.

Discussion Questions

If you are leading a Support Group or want to Journal while reading this book, you may use these thought provoking questions to apply what you are reading. Grief is in many stages and processing your thinking helps you move through those stages. Use these questions to help you on your journey.

1. What impacted you the most from this chapter?

2. Which aspect of the story touched you the most?

3. What about this child's life is going to be a legacy to their life - positive or negative?

4. Does this in any way inspire you to live differently?

5. Was there anything that prepared the family to cope with this tragic event?

6. What have you learned from the mother or circumstances that can help you deal with loss?

7. What did the mother and family do to move forward?

8. What "Take Away" can you apply to your own life?

Acknowledgements

The birthing process of a book requires the support and encouragement of an incredible cast of family, friends and personal cheerleaders. First and foremost on my gratitude list are the brave mothers whose stories had to be told. How many boxes of Kleenex were required by mother and writer was not tallied, but through the tears each mother wanted her child's death to be a stepping stone for another family's healing journey.

My husband Larry's patient encouragement along my three year endurance race, or I should say "walk," was priceless. My sister Patti Hoffman's hours of proofing and creative support were invaluable, along with my business assistant Ginna Olsen. My professional editors' work by Renee Broadwell and editor, Mike Yorkey brought the book to life with polish.

The Lord brought into my life numbers of girlfriends who shared the devastation of their child's death to inspire me to bring hope to others' lives: Vicki Serles loss of David; Cheryl William's precious Brittany; Janette Henning, my website creator's beautiful daughter Melissa; my dearest friend Kay Davis who lost not only beautiful Heather but her husband Jeff a year later; and my daughter-in-law Tina's baby Arri and her mother Margie's loss of Tina's sister, Kaesy.

Within the sisterhood of grieving mothers is an incredible support community. The Umbrella Ministries San Diego moms call each other, walk together, listen to each other over coffee, shop together as they once did with their teen daughters. Not one of us wants to be in the group but by coming together we have found strength and renewed joy even with a gaping hole in our lives.

Standing out as my number one cheerleader is Marcia Ramsland known as "The Organizing Pro." That she is and more. Marcia, a successful writer of seven books, never gave up on me through three years of fitful writing. Life often got in my way taking me along family and professional detours that precluded time for writing. Marcia never gave up. Formulating deadlines, sparking a renewed interest with future target events where the book could be spotlighted, she persisted to the finish line and then stuck with me through the decisions for the title, cover, editing, proofing and finally publishing. Marcia, your personal commitment to me was a driving force for the book's completion. I'm singing your praises everyday.

The glory and honor for this book belongs to my Heavenly Father, the God of all comfort, who touched my life and the lives of these mothers. My training and board participation with *Lead Like Jesus* developed within me the habits and the mind of Christ that allowed me to reflect His heart for the hurting and become His hands of practical comfort to those around me.

My FaithWalk small group, reflecting the principles of *Lead Like Jesus,* prayed me through the creation of this book. Thank you Margie Blanchard, Sherry Hougard, Audrey Coleman, Jeannie Abts, Charlie Littrell and Liz Buenrostro for your faithful prayers and confidence in me.

To my extended family who for three years lived through their mother and grandmother being unavailable on various "writing" weekends, I appreciate your patience. This is a book whose purpose you couldn't quite understand. Your Mimi loves each one of you: Ben, Jesse, Solomon, Job and baby Abraham. And to my precious

Madelyn, who is becoming an avid reader, I pray these stories will encourage your faith in God and His incredible love for you.

Every stumbling block along the way convinced me that there was a power present in this world that did not want hope to be spoken into the lives of brokenhearted people. God has the victory. With *Hope for a Broken Heart* in your hands you too can be an instrument used by God to bring His power of healing into the crushed lives of those he causes to cross your path.

It is a God-moment that you have read this book. Be alert to how He is going to use you for His greater good. We are in this world to serve Him. To God be the glory.

— Linda D. Stirling

About the Author

Linda D. Stirling is a gifted communicator with years of experience coming alongside grieving mothers at the lowest moments of their lives. The process of healing from the death of a child, she says, is a lifelong journey, and the true stories in *Hope for a Broken Heart* chronicle the journeys that each mother traveled toward a renewed purpose in life.

My friendship with another group of Christian women led to the formation of the San Diego chapter of The Professional Women's Fellowship, an organization that brings together women of all occupations to network and support one another at monthly meetings. My presentation to this group on **The Shepherd's Walk** led to the writing of an article by the same title which was then included in my church's monthly periodical. Coupled with the hope-filled stories heard at Umbrella Ministries meetings the creation of *Hope for the Broken Heart* became a reality.

Linda is currently a Senior Vice President, Wealth Management Advisor with UBS Financial Services in San Diego and Sun Valley, Idaho, where she works with her surviving son Greg. Linda has repeatedly joined the ranks of Barron's Top 100 Women Advisors in America. She makes her home in San Diego, where she lives with her husband of 22 years, former California State Senator and retired judge Larry Stirling. She and Larry enjoy their special time with five grandsons and one granddaughter.

Resources

Invite Linda Stirling to Speak
to Your Community Organization or Grief Group

Linda D. Stirling is a dynamic speaker whose presentation, "Walking Out of the Valley of the Shadow," has received accolades from audiences large and small. She also teaches others what it means to take control of their financial future. She has been a featured speaker for Merrill Lynch and RBC Wealth Management as well as a contributor to financial periodicals.

If you or your Community Group or Grief Organization would like to ask Linda for a speaking engagement, contact her through her website at www.hopeforabrokenheart.com.

Book Purchases

For bulk purchases of *Hope for a Broken Heart*, you may order them at a discount through Linda's website www.hopeforabrokenheart. com.

Hope for a Broken Heart is for . . .

- Parents who have experienced the death of a child
- A friend caught in the fog of grief and depression
- Family and others who want to understand and bring comfort
- Support Groups on the healing journey
- Health Care Professionals and Counselors who reach families

If this book has been of help to you, please do write and let us know. I'd love to hear from you.

Sincerely,

Linda D. Stirling

www.hopeforabrokenheart.com

"And our hope for you is firm,
because we know that just as you share in our sufferings,
so also you share in our comfort."

II Corinthians 1:7 (NIV)